GOOD MEALS
ON A SMALL BUDGET

GOOD MEALS
ON A SMALL BUDGET

by Gladys Mann

HAMLYN
LONDON · NEW YORK · SYDNEY · TORONTO

Published by
The Hamlyn Publishing Group Limited
London · New York · Sydney · Toronto
Hamlyn House, Feltham, Middlesex, England

© Copyright The Hamlyn Publishing Group Limited 1969
ISBN 0 600 03434 8

First published 1969
Reprinted 1970

Printed in England by Petty and Sons Limited, Leeds

Contents

Introduction

What is a GOOD MEAL?

A Good Meal should be appetising, enjoyable, attractively served and satisfying; it should be nourishing, well-balanced, containing all the constituents necessary for health, growth, development and tissue repair, and general well-being. It should be well flavoured and seasoned, but not so highly seasoned and artificially flavoured that the natural flavour of the food is killed.

A Good Meal is not necessarily the most expensive meal. If you have to feed your family on a small budget, don't think that meals are bound to be unappetising, monotonous and dull, or lacking in flavour and nourishment, or that your family will be underfed.

In fact there are dietitians and nutritional experts who say there is more malnutrition among rich people than among those with moderate incomes. In other words, fancy, expensive, rich foods do not always contain all the food constituents necessary for a healthy body. This is particularly true where children and adolescents are concerned, youngsters who need plenty of plain, 'filling' foods, rich in proteins for growth and energy.

There is no need here to go into an intricate study of all the food constituents the body requires. All you need remember is that everybody needs protein, fat, carbohydrates, vitamins and minerals every day. I have tried to vary the recipes in this book to make sure you can give your family all that is necessary for a well-balanced diet, and at the same time give them good, interesting meals at low cost.

> All recipes are for 4 generous servings, with one or two exceptions which are given. If your family is smaller or larger than this you will need to adjust the quantities to the most economical amount for the number you have to budget for.

Some Useful Facts and Figures

Comparison of Weights and Measures

English weights and measures have been used throughout the book. 3 teaspoonfuls equal 1 tablespoon. The average English teacup is ¼ pint. The average English breakfast cup is ½ pint. When cups are mentioned in recipes they refer to a B.S.I. measuring cup which holds ½ pint or 10 fluid ounces. In case it is wished to translate quantities into American or metric counterparts the following give a comparison.

Liquid measure

The American pint is 16 fluid ounces, as opposed to the British Imperial pint and Canadian pint which are 20 fluid ounces. The American ½-pint measuring cup is therefore equivalent to ⅖ British pint. In Australia the British Imperial pint, 20 fluid ounces, is used.

Solid measure

British	American
1 lb. butter or other fat	2 cups
1 lb. flour	4 cups
1 lb. granulated or castor sugar	2 cups
1 lb. icing or confectioners' sugar	3 cups
1 lb. brown (moist) sugar	2½ cups
1 lb. golden syrup or treacle	1 cup
1 lb. rice	2 cups
1 lb. dried fruit	2 cups
1 lb. chopped meat (finely packed)	2 cups
1 lb. lentils or split peas	2 cups
1 lb. coffee (unground)	2½ cups
1 lb. soft breadcrumbs	4 cups
½ oz. flour	1 level tablespoon
1 oz. flour	1 heaped tablespoon
1 oz. sugar	1 level tablespoon
½ oz. butter	1 level tablespoon, smoothed off
1 oz. golden syrup or treacle	1 level tablespoon
1 oz. jam or jelly	1 level tablespoon

All U.S. standard measuring tablespoons

To help you understand metrication

You will see from the chart that 1 oz. is approximately 28 g. but can be rounded off to the more convenient measuring unit of 25. Also the figures in the right hand column are not always increased by 25. This is to reduce the difference between the convenient number and the nearest equivalent. If in a recipe the ingredients to be converted are 1 oz. of margarine and 6 oz. of flour, these are the conversions: 25 g. margarine and 175 g. flour.

The conversion chart

Ounces	Approx. g. and ml. to nearest whole number	Approx. to nearest unit of 25
1	28	25
2	57	50
3	85	75
4	113	125
5	142	150
6	170	175
7	198	200
8	226	225
12	340	350
16	456	450

Note: When converting quantities over 16 oz. first add the appropriate figures in the centre column, not those given in the right hand column, THEN adjust to the nearest unit of 25g. For example, to convert 1¾ lb. add 456 g. to 340 g. which equals 796 g. When rounded off to the convenient figure it becomes 800 g.

Approximate liquid conversions

¼ pint–150 ml.   *1,000 millilitres–1 l (litre)
½ pint–275 ml.   1 l–1¾ pints
¾ pint–425 ml.   ½ l–¾ pint plus 4 tablespoons
1 pint–575 ml.   1 dl. (decilitre)–6 tablespoons

Note: If solid ingredients give scant weight using the 25 unit conversion, the amount of liquid allowed must also be scant. For example, although 575 ml. is nearer to 1 pint (20 fluid oz.) when making a white pouring sauce use 550 ml. of milk to 25 g. each of butter and flour for a better consistency.

Oven Temperatures

The following chart gives conversions from degrees Fahrenheit to degrees Celsius (formerly known as Centigrade). This chart is accurate to within 3° Celsius, and can therefore be used for recipes which give oven temperatures in metric.

Description	Electric Setting	Gas Mark
very cool	225°F–110°C	$\frac{1}{4}$
	250°F–130°C	$\frac{1}{2}$
cool	275°F–140°C	1
	300°F–150°C	2
moderate	325°F–170°C	3
	350°F–180°C	4
moderately hot	375°F–190°C	5
	400°F–200°C	6
hot	425°F–220°C	7
	450°F–230°C	8
very hot	475°F–240°C	9

Note: This table is an approximate guide only. Different makes of cooker vary and if you are in any doubt about the setting it is as well to refer to the manufacturer's temperature chart.

The Food We Need

Foods rich in high quality protein are meat, fish, eggs and cheese. Milk, nuts and some vegetables contain protein, but it is not of high quality. The cheap cuts of meat, cheap fish and the cheapest cheese have just the same quality protein as the most expensive varieties. Offal – liver, heart, kidneys also contain protein and iron. Ox liver and kidney are rich in protein and iron and are cheaper than sheep, lamb or pork offal.

Fats are important because they contain a lot of calories, necessary for warmth and energy. Here again the cheapest form of fat has just the same quality protein as the most expensive – the food value of margarine is as good as that of butter, and ordinary lard is just as good as the modern 'refined' fats lightened with whipped-up vegetable oils. Suet and dripping are rich in calories.

Carbohydrates supply energy and extra calories. Potatoes, pastas and bread are the cheapest source, but all sweet and starchy foods come under this group. Carbohydrate foods are good fillers for children. However, it is better to supply their needs from potatoes, bread, pastas and puddings rather than very sticky cakes and biscuits. Carbohydrates encourage weight increase in adults.

Vitamins and minerals are needed in the diet. However, a healthy person eating a regular balanced diet will automatically take in as many of these as necessary.

In a nut-shell, a well-balanced diet should include daily:–

1 Milk; children 1 pint, adults $\frac{1}{2}$ to $\frac{3}{4}$ pint. This can include milk used in beverages, in cooking and with cereals.
2 Meat, bacon, or fish. Once a week liver or kidney.
3 Egg – 'neat' or in a made-up dish; cheese.
4 Un-fired food, such as salad, tomatoes, fruit – especially oranges.
5 Green vegetables and potatoes. Rice, pasta, pulse vegetables (dried peas, beans of all kinds) can take the place of, or be served in addition to, potatoes.
6 Bread and cereals.

7 Butter or margarine, lard, oil or cooking fat as required. Suet used in puddings, or dripping used in frying can make up part of the fat quota.

8 In the case of children, fresh fruit juice, or bottled black-currant juice or rose-hip syrup. Avoid expensive, over-sugared, synthetic bottled fruit drinks or commercial flavoured drinks.

If you enjoy cooking and have no other calls on your time outside your home, I do urge you to buy the ingredients and make your own cakes, biscuits, pastries and pies. Honestly, I don't know how the woman with a small budget and perhaps two or three hungry youngsters, can manage to buy shop cakes, etc. – 2s. 6d. or 3s. for a cake that disappears at one meal. The same money would produce a cake twice the size, taste better and be more nourishing. Scones, buns and tartlets, too – the price is staggering and they are so easy to make.

The same with jams and pickles and other preserves. I am appalled at the prices in the shops. Even if you don't grow you own fruit it would pay you when certain fruits are in season to make your own jam. I have included in this book some 'can't fail' recipes for simple jams, pickles and chutneys, and I do hope you will try them; they will help you to keep a better table within your budget.

Cold meats too – they're expensive to buy, but so useful for supper or high tea, or when you haven't time to cook. Why not try your hand at making your own? Many can be made from the cheapest cuts, or offal, and the flavour is much better than the bought ready-cooked kinds.

Shopping-wise

Good meals begin with good shopping, no matter how much or how little you have to spend. It is absolutely essential if you have a limited, small budget, to shop wisely. Have a basic plan, and stick to it, but be prepared to alter your meal plans if you see any real bargains going. Don't indulge in 'impulse' buying, or be led astray by 'special offers' unless you can see a real use for them.

You will save money, time and worry if you:

1 Plan your menus, at least for the main meal, for a week ahead. There is less risk of untidy left-overs if you do this, and you can buy on one shopping-trip ingredients that will supplement each other in your meal planning.

2 Check your store cupboard to see if any basic items are missing – such as salt, pepper, flour, sugar, mustard, vinegar, oil, bottled sauce – things that are so often overlooked until the last grain or drop is used. Replenish as soon as they get low.

3 As a rule it is cheaper to buy large sizes. But have a care – a large size may tempt you or your family to be over-generous in the use of its contents. And don't buy large sizes of foodstuffs that you are not likely to use up in a reasonable time; many things go 'off' quickly once the packet is opened.

4 Foods in season (chiefly fruit and vegetables), have a better flavour as well as being cheaper. Any food that goes scarce because of the season or weather conditions (such as fish) becomes dear, so you should be prepared to change your food plan if you included such items.

5 Look out for shops that have cut prices for well-known branded goods, but beware of unknown or obviously shop-soiled 'bargains'.

6 Try each week to buy something that will keep well in cool cupboard or fridge but which you do not need for immediate use, and so build up a reserve for emergencies or special occasions. Most canned goods keep for weeks or months. With this in mind you are quite justified in buying the occasional tin of meat, fish or fruit, items which I would not encourage anyone with a low budget to buy for everyday use.

7 If you shop early in the day you get a better choice, but if you know that in your district prices are reduced for perishables, then you can save money by shopping late. This often applies in country districts in the soft fruit season, or where locally grown produce is on sale.

At the Butcher

There are many meat dishes that taste just as good, or even better if made from the lower priced cuts rather than the expensive cuts. It is more a matter of careful planning and shopping and method of cooking than of cost. If I had all the money in the world, I wouldn't buy the best rump steak and lambs' kidneys for making a steak and kidney pudding or for a casserole.

The fact is, that for a dish requiring long, slow cooking the cheaper stewing meat is more suitable and tastes just as good.

Don't 'turn up your nose' at the parts of meat known by the rather nasty word, offal – the innards of animals. The real gourmet knows well what delicious meals they make; you on your small budget will soon learn that they are comparatively cheap and good to eat. There is one liver that comes in the luxury class – calves' liver, so you'll steer away from that. Not that you're likely to be tempted to buy it; what there is goes to the better restaurants and rarely reaches the ordinary butcher.

Since meat of any kind is the most expensive item in any budget, it is worth while to shop around until you find the butcher who understands and appreciates your needs. Tell him exactly how you want to cook the meat, how much you want, or can pay for it, within a copper or two. Beware of the butcher who can never, but never, cut you a joint to the weight you ask (it is always over, never under); who always has his joints neatly trimmed, de-boned and rolled, so there is no way of telling whether the pieces named top-side, top-rump, silver-side, etc., really are those cuts. Did you know that meat bought on the bone *should* be cheaper than that ready boned and tortured into a neat shape? All right – you can't eat bones, but meat tastes better if roasted on the bone; if you insist on having the joint cut from the carcass you can see what you are buying, and you can always ask the butcher to bone it for you after weighing, if you must. And do take the bones home to simmer, with a few root vegetables added, for gravy or stock. Believe me, I have heard women refuse the bones, and giblets of chicken, and seen in their baskets: canned soups and baby foods, and vegetables and bouillon cubes. Very convenient and good, no doubt, but costly items if you have to provide good meals on a small budget.

Don't insist on having your joints with practically no fat. I know many people think fat is wasteful, but you can't have really tender, juicy meat without a fair proportion of fat. You have to add fat of some kind if there is none on the meat – more expense. And what about real roast dripping, especially beef? I can remember the joy of hot toast and beef dripping for breakfast or tea on a winter's day. And what a saving on butter with a family.

When you want minced beef, buy the meat in the piece, so you can be sure there is not too much fat, gristle or skin; then ask the butcher to put it through his mincer. *Never* buy ready minced meat unless you can absolutely trust your butcher.

When buying lamb, insist that the butcher remove the tough outer skin. This applies more to imported lamb (which is often small mutton) than to English. With English lamb the skin may be too fine and tender to remove; in this case it should be slashed diagonally, so that it does not get 'drawn up' during roasting. *Do* pester your butcher, if need be, to let you have your pork with the rind on, even if it means having a slightly fatter joint. What is pork without crackling? I know my family thinks it the best part of the joint. And if you get a little extra fat, well, pork dripping is as good as, if not better than, cooking fat in pastry for savoury pies, and for frying, so there is really no loss. Be sure the rind is well scored by the butcher.

At the Fishmonger

Many women who have to make good meals on a small budget say they can't have fish very often, because it is too dear to buy enough to satisfy the appetites of a healthy family. Well, so it is, if you always insist on buying the most expensive (not necessarily the best) fish, and serve it as often as not just fried or boiled with a few potatoes. Many kinds of fish that are inclined to be tasteless are improved if cooked with, or at least served with, the vegetables we as a matter of course serve with meat dishes. Leaving aside the popular and expensive fish such as sole, plaice, turbot, halibut, hake, salmon or trout, there are at least a dozen other fish to choose from, as well flavoured, and better for 'made-up' dishes, as the expensive kinds: haddock and whiting, the 'chicken of the sea' though the bones are a nuisance; cod, sometimes tasteless, but ideal for casseroles or fish pies; gurnet, as firm and meaty as halibut; eels; sea bream, under its tough skin as delicious as expensive trout or mullet; skate, though this is getting more expensive on account of scarcity.

Then there are those anonymous 'white fillets', a name which covers a number of fish species, which if the housewife saw with their heads, skins and tails on, she would be put off by their ugliness: cat-fish, dog-fish, monk-fish particularly. If the fish fillets have no skin on you may be sure they are one of these fishes. They are quite good and palatable but should not be sold as cod or haddock fillets – in fact, in law it is forbidden to do so.

And what about herrings, mackerel, and sprats? The fish that, when in season, are relatively cheap, very nutritious and delicious.

Make the most use of them when you can – and they *must* be eaten in season to be at their best. Herrings are at their best during May and June when their fat content is at the highest; they are good all summer but the fat content falls gradually; sprats are in season from October to March and are very cheap and make a delicious meal grilled, or fried, or oven-baked and served with mustard sauce.

Mackerel are at their best in April, May, June and early July. They are the most perishable fish and should be eaten as quickly as possible after being caught, especially in hot weather. Herrings, mackerel and sprats are very tasty eaten cold, soused or plain baked; they are excellent for summer cold meals when they are in season.

Smoked fish – kippered herrings, smoked haddock, smoked sprats, bloaters (often hard to come by) – used to be one of the cheapest foods, but they have gradually become dearer, chiefly because of the labour involved in processing them. But they are still a relatively cheap food and very, very appetising. When eggs are cheap: 'Egg and Haddie' high-tea or supper is really a treat – a great favourite in the North. Golden fillets, often of an unknown species are usually dearer than the real haddock, and to my mind not nearly so tasty; children seem to like them, probably because they are boneless and the colour is attractive.

At the Grocer

To my mind, the grocers' shops or supermarkets are the biggest snare for the housewife who must shop on a small budget. Here, all your best-laid plans can go haywire if you don't watch out. Take a firm grip on your shopping list and stick to the basics: tea, coffee, instant or ground, sugar, flour, butter, margarine, cooking fat or cooking oil, vinegar and other seasonings and flavourings, pasta and rice, cornflakes or other cereals, cake fruits and biscuits, jellies, jams, marmalade (if you don't make your own) or honey, Marmite or other favourite spread, bacon, cheese, eggs. It won't, perhaps, be necessary to buy all these things every week; in fact I find it a saving in time and the few odd coppers here and there, to shop for non-perishables such as sugar, flour, rice and pastas, cereals and preserves once a month. The only drawback to this is the extra weight to carry if you haven't a car or if the shops don't deliver. This is where the family can be a help on a shopping expedition. Children usually find it great fun.

Having got your basic groceries, you *might* have something to spare for items in the canned line that you know your family likes, or to add to your store cupboard. A can of condensed soup can be a good buy; and my children used to give squeals of delight if I produced a tin of baked beans – probably because I never used canned vegetables except as a last resort. A good thing to have in store is canned, diced mixed vegetables (cost about 1s.); with some stock or a bouillon cube you have the makings of a quick soup. Bouillon cubes and gravy mixes, by the way, can be life-savers on many occasions for quick gravies and sauces, and they keep a long time. Dehydrated vegetables are easy to carry and to store, have good flavour and keep almost indefinitely.

At the Fruiterer and Greengrocer

Here you certainly want your wits about you. Have a good look round before you start to buy, noting carefully quality as well as price; in the supermarket where everything is pre-packed it is not always easy to see the damaged tomato in the pack, or judge whether the greens are going soft in the middle, but at least you have the chance to pick out what you want. On the other hand, in a shop with a man to serve you it is amazing how often he manages by some sleight of hand to slip in the damaged fruit or faded greens that all looked so good from the front.

Shun the fruiterer or greengrocer who won't let you have the goods of your choice. This applies particularly to Brussels sprouts, tomatoes, cauliflowers, greens, apples, bananas, grapes, lettuce. Of course, they spend a lot of time making a beautiful display to catch your eye, but they show righteous indignation if you insist on wanting the things from the front of the picture, and as for picking out your own, that really upsets them. You can admire but not touch. Never mind; point to the cabbage, cauliflower, lettuce, the bunch of grapes you want; insist that you get at least some of the sprouts from the front of the pile; reject the apples with obvious bruises. When buying strawberries in punnets, shake the punnet gently so that you can see if there are any bad ones underneath. No one should have to pay dearly for uneatable goods, particularly when you are shopping on a small budget.

When shopping for vegetables you can save yourself time and trouble if you think ahead to the main dishes you have planned for the week; for instance, if you are going to casserole or stew the remains of the joint see that you have the onions, carrots, turnips, outer stalks of celery that you will require.

Soups on a Small Budget

Thick meaty or vegetable soups are ideal, cheap 'fillers-up' when you have to cater on a small budget. These hearty soups, especially when they contain pieces of meat or bacon or dumplings and are served with chopped hard-boiled egg, or pancake or grated cheese garnish, can well form the main part of the meal if there is a satisfying pudding to follow.

It is not necessary to have specially made stock for making these soups, though it is an improvement. Chicken or beef bouillon cubes are excellent substitutes for home-made stock. Never throw away even cooked bones without first boiling them to extract the last scrap of goodness and flavour from them; vegetable water (except potato water) should be saved for soup. Bacon rinds and bones give a good flavour to soup; they should be removed before serving the soup. A knuckle of shank end of veal or bacon, boiled in the soup but taken out before it gets 'ragged', the meat removed from the bones, can be served separately. Return the bones to the soup pan.

Lentil Soup with Chopped Egg

you will need:

6 oz. red lentils	a bacon bone, or a few
4 pints water	rinds
1 large onion	$\frac{1}{2}$ teaspoon salt
1 large carrot	$\frac{1}{4}$ teaspoon pepper
2 large potatoes	2 hard-boiled eggs
bouquet garni (see page 19)	$\frac{1}{4}$ pint milk
1 oz. dripping	chopped parsley

1 Wash lentils, wash and peel vegetables and cut into small pieces.
2 Put all, except potatoes, into a thick pan with the dripping, bacon bone or rinds and bouquet garni. Cook gently over low heat for 5 minutes, shaking pan often to prevent sticking.
3 Add water, salt and pepper and simmer 1 hour. Remove rind or bone.
4 Add potatoes and simmer, stirring often until reduced to a pulp. Rub through hair or nylon sieve.
5 Add milk to purée, boil up, taste and add more salt and pepper if necessary. Pour into four bowls.
6 Chop cold hard-boiled eggs until crumbly, put a pile in centre of each soup bowl; sprinkle chopped parsley on top.

Beef Broth with Parsley Dumplings

you will need:

8 oz. shin of beef	medium-sized turnip
2 pints water or	stalk of celery
vegetable stock	1 oz. dripping
1 teaspoon salt	chopped parsley for
$\frac{1}{4}$ teaspoon pepper	garnish
1 carrot	Parsley Dumplings
1 onion	

1 Wash meat, cut into small pieces, removing any skin.
2 Put in large pan with water or stock, add salt and pepper; simmer 1 hour.
3 Wash, peel and dice vegetables; heat dripping and fry vegetables for a few minutes, stirring often.
4 When meat has simmered 1 hour add lightly fried vegetables; simmer until they are cooked, 40 minutes to 1 hour.
5 Add Parsley Dumplings 20 minutes before soup is done. Sprinkle chopped parsley on soup when serving.

For the Dumplings

4 oz. self-raising flour	1 dessertspoon chopped
2 oz. shredded suet	parsley
$\frac{1}{4}$ teaspoon salt	

Mix dry ingredients; form into soft dough with cold water. Form into small balls on floured board. Cook 20 minutes.

Lancashire Soup

you will need:

8 oz. sheep's liver	2 oz. margarine or
8 oz. bacon bones, or	pork dripping
trimmings and rinds	1 medium sized onion
3 pints stock, or beef	1 oz. flour
bouillon cubes mixed	2 slices stale bread
with water	salt and pepper
	toast croûtons

1 Wash and wipe the liver, removing skin and any gristly tubes. Remove surplus fat from bacon trimmings.
2 Put liver and bacon trimmings, bones and rinds, in large pan with the stock; bring to the boil.

3 Melt margarine or dripping, add onion and fry until a good brown. Stir in the flour and let it brown slightly.
4 Add blended flour and onion to boiling stock, etc. Boil for 30 minutes; remove bacon bones and rinds, if used.
5 Add bread cut into squares, simmer 5 minutes or until bread is soft.
6 Rub the soup through a coarse sieve or Mouli grater. Reheat to boiling point. Taste and season carefully – bacon may make the soup salty. Serve with toast croûtons.

To make the Croûtons: Use ready-sliced bread. Remove crusts from slices. Cut slices in halves diagonally. Place on a baking sheet in a medium oven until slices are a pale biscuit colour and quite crisp and curly at the corners.

French Onion Soup

you will need:

1 lb. onions	salt and black pepper
3 oz. best margarine	French bread cut into
1 tablespoon flour	$\frac{3}{4}$-inch slices
3 pints brown stock or	6 oz. Cheddar cheese
dissolved beef bouillon cubes	

1 Slice onions thinly; heat margarine in soup pan and fry onions until golden.
2 Sprinkle in the flour and stir until smooth and slightly browned.
3 Add stock or bouillon slowly, stirring constantly until smooth. Season with salt and pepper. Simmer 15 minutes.
4 Allow three slices French bread per person. Cover each slice with thinly sliced cheese.
5 Pour soup into a wide earthenware dish. Float the cheese-covered slices on top. Cover dish and leave in warm place for 5 minutes.
6 Place uncovered dish under red hot grill, not too near the heat, until cheese browns slightly. Serve at once.

Cream of Chicken Soup

you will need:

1 pint chicken stock from boiling chicken, or chicken cube	salt and pepper
	2 egg yolks
1 pint milk	1 tablespoon top of milk or
2 oz. finest semolina	evaporated milk
$\frac{1}{2}$ teaspoon made mustard	crisp bacon garnish

1 Heat stock and milk. Pour in the semolina slowly, stirring until mixture comes to the boil.
2 Add mustard, salt and pepper. Beat egg yolks.
3 Beat $\frac{1}{4}$ pint of the soup into the egg yolks, mix well, and whisk mixture into the soup. Add top of milk or evaporated milk, mix well but do not allow to boil again.
4 Pour into four heated soup bowls. Sprinkle crisp bacon garnish on tops.

To make the Garnish: Remove rinds and brown edges from 4 rashers of streaky bacon. With scissors cut bacon into $\frac{1}{4}$-inch strips, put in a shallow tin under heated grill until brown and crisp. Put on to kitchen paper to absorb fat, then sprinkle over the soup.

Almond Garnish: Blanch 1 oz. almonds, by pouring boiling water over them, when skins can be slipped off. Chop the almonds finely and sprinkle on top of soup or on top of separate helpings.

Chicken Carcass left from roast or boiled chicken can be added to the soup, and all scraps of meat removed from bones and returned to the soup after cooking; also use any chicken giblets.

Pea Soup

you will need:

$\frac{1}{2}$ pint dried green split peas	1 outside stalk celery
	level tablespoon flour
4 pints water in which bacon has been boiled, or a few bacon bones added to plain water	pepper
	salt if required; ham or bacon water will be salty
1 large onion	2 teaspoons dried mint, or
1 large carrot	$\frac{1}{2}$ tablespoon chopped fresh mint

1 Soak the peas overnight. Strain and put into pan with water; bring to the boil.
2 Chop vegetables, add to the stock and simmer 2 hours.
3 Rub through a sieve and return all to pan, except bones if used.
4 Mix flour to a smooth paste with a little stock and add to the purée; simmer 3 to 4 minutes. Season as required.
5 Put dried mint or chopped mint in bottom of tureen and pour the soup over it.
A knob of butter or margarine stirred in is an improvement.
For Haricot Bean Soup substitute 8 oz. haricot beans for the split peas, and chopped parsley instead of mint.

Minestrone

you will need:

8 oz. mixed vegetables (carrot, onion, celery, cabbage)	clove of garlic or $\frac{1}{4}$ teaspoon garlic salt
1 oz. pork dripping or margarine	level tablespoon rice
1½ pints stock or water	2 tablespoons tomato ketchup
1 oz. macaroni	1 teaspoon chopped parsley
1 oz. cooked haricot beans	grated cheese

1 Slice or dice the vegetables and cook for 10 minutes in the fat without browning.
2 Add stock, bring to the boil; add macaroni, beans, garlic or garlic salt, boil 30 minutes.
3 Add the rice and the ketchup, salt and pepper to taste and cook for a further 30 minutes, then add the parsley.
4 Serve very hot, with grated cheese handed separately.

Leek and Potato Soup

you will need:

4 oz. pork dripping or margarine	2 sprigs parsley
4 medium sized leeks	1 stalk celery
1 onion	2 large potatoes
2 pints stock or dissolved chicken bouillon cubes	salt and pepper
	grating of nutmeg
	1 tablespoon top of milk

1 Melt fat, finely slice white part of leeks; dice onion, add to the fat and cook gently 5–8 minutes.
2 Add stock, chopped parsley, potatoes cut into dice, and chopped celery.
3 Cook until potatoes are tender, then rub through sieve. Season with salt and pepper and grating of nutmeg.
4 Just before serving add tablespoon top of milk.

This soup may be left to go cold, then chilled in fridge overnight. Sprinkle with finely chopped chives and this is now that favourite summer-time soup, **Crème Vichyssoise.**

Cheese Soup

you will need:

2 oz. butter or margarine	$\frac{1}{2}$ teaspoon salt
4 oz. finely chopped onion	$\frac{1}{4}$ teaspoon pepper
1 pint hot white stock or vegetable water or plain water	1 teaspoon chopped parsley
$\frac{1}{2}$ pint milk	4 oz. grated stale cheese
2 tablespoons flour	crushed cream cracker crumbs

1 Heat fat in soup pan, add the onion and fry it until transparent but not brown.
2 Add the hot stock or water and simmer 10 minutes; then add the milk.
3 Mix the flour to a smooth paste with a little extra milk, add to the pan slowly stirring all the time until boiling again.
4 Add salt and pepper and parsley; cook and stir 5 minutes.
5 Add the cheese, stir and boil up again. Serve very hot. Pour into hot soup bowls and sprinkle crushed cream cracker crumbs on top.

For Green Spinach Soup: use half the quantity of grated cheese and add 2 tablespoons chopped cooked spinach; garnish with chopped green parts of spring onions.

Marrow Soup

you will need:

1 large marrow	1½ oz. flour
3 oz. butter or margarine	$\frac{1}{2}$ pint milk
1 small sliced onion	1 egg yolk
$\frac{1}{2}$ pint water	2 tablespoons top milk or evaporated milk
bouquet garni (see page 19)	fried bread or toast
$\frac{1}{2}$ teaspoon salt	
$\frac{1}{4}$ teaspoon white pepper	

1 Peel marrow, cut in pieces, removing seeds.
2 Melt butter in saucepan, add the marrow and sliced onion; cook for 5 minutes, stirring well.
3 Add the water, *bouquet garni*, salt and pepper; simmer until marrow is quite soft.
4 Strain through sieve; mash the marrow until smooth, add to liquid and return to saucepan; place over low heat.
5 Blend flour smoothly with the milk, add to the marrow purée, bring to the boil, simmer 5 minutes.
6 Blend yolk of egg with cream or evaporated milk, stir it into the soup, reheat, but do not allow to boil.
7 Serve with croûtons of bread fried in butter, or thin toast.

Fish on a Small Budget

Fish for the main dish on a small budget means that you must stick to the coarser, more substantial type of fish rather than the more delicate kinds that are not only more expensive but are not nearly so filling – which is an important consideration when you have several hungry people to feed.

The cheaper fish such as cod or haddock, or sea bream are best fried or oven-baked; herrings and mackerel, cheapest fish of all, soused and left to go cold are good stand-bys for breakfast, high tea or supper.

Smell and appearance are the best guides when buying fish. There should be no unpleasant smell; the eyes should be bright and not sunken, and the tail end stiff yet springy; fillets should have a creamy opaque look; not watery looking. When buying fillets of cod or haddock, look at the skin side; the skin of cod is a pale, blueish-grey fading to white at the edge that was the underside of the whole fish; haddock is a paler grey and has a dark line running down the middle. The skin of herrings and mackerel should be bright, almost iridescent, and the markings quite clear and defined.

It is usually cheaper to buy cod or haddock in the piece; a tail end of cod, for instance, is cheaper than two fillets, and for baking or casseroling the flavour is better if the fish is cooked on the bone. If you want fillets it is quite easy to bone the fish yourself, and you can boil the fish bone for making sauce. Small whole haddocks weighing 2–3 lb. are a good buy when you have several people to cater for, and they are excellent stuffed and baked whole. Sea bream is another firm, round fish that is ideal for baking, stuffed or unstuffed; it has very thick and tough scales, very hard to remove; the fishmonger will usually do this for you, though for baking I find it is better to leave the fish unscaled and remove skin and scales together after baking. This also helps to keep in the flavour of the fish. Gurnet is another cheap fish, with a large (in proportion to its body) ugly head and a lovely delicate pinkish skin; its flesh is firm and white and has a good, 'unfishy' flavour. It is best stuffed and baked.

There is little good to be said about the boiling of fish; if you can get really fresh cod there may be something to be said for Boiled Cod and Parsley Sauce, but even so, steaming is better than boiling, and a strong-flavoured, spicy sauce is an improvement.

To Deep Fry Fish: Small fillets from tail end of cod or haddock should be used. If large cut in halves. Wash and dry thoroughly. Have heating a deep pan of lard, clarified dripping or cooking oil. Put beaten egg on a plate; brush pieces of fish with it. Put dry, fine white breadcrumbs on piece of soft paper; toss the egged fish in these, lifting the ends of the paper up and down so fish is covered with the crumbs. Shake fish to remove loose crumbs; put the pieces in a frying basket in one layer. Lower gently into smoking hot fat, which must be deep enough to cover the fish. Lower heat for first 2 or 3 minutes then increase it slowly and fry the fish a further 8 to 10 minutes according to thickness of fish. Fish should be a good golden brown. Allow surplus fat to drip from fish in basket, then drain on kitchen paper; serve as soon as possible.

To Shallow Fry Fish: Use a thick aluminium frying pan. Heat fat, to the depth of half an inch. Dry fish, dip in milk or egg and milk, then in seasoned flour. Shake off surplus; leave for 5–10 minutes, then dip again in seasoned flour. Shake off surplus. When fat is hot, put in fish, fry until brown on under-side, turn and fry on second side. Fat should come halfway up fish pieces. Drain well; serve very hot.

To Grill Fish: Have the grill red hot. Wash and dry fillets or thin slices of cod or haddock; brush over both sides with melted butter, margarine or cooking oil, place on grid in grill pan, put pan under grill about 2 inches away from the burners or elements of grill. Grill 5–8 minutes according to thickness of fish, then turn and grill for the same length of time on second side, taking care fish does not get blackened. Grilled fish does not need to drain, as it is not immersed in fat. Serve very hot with a sharp sauce, such as tartare (see page 49).

To Steam Fish: Small pieces can be steamed in an ordinary vegetable steamer. Season the fish with salt and pepper and a good squeeze of lemon juice. The boiling water in the pan should be seasoned with salt, peppercorns and vinegar (a tablespoon to the pint). Place fish in upper part of steamer and steam 15 to 20 minutes according to thickness. Test with a fork for readiness; it should flake easily. Take up carefully; put on to hot dish and coat with any well-seasoned sauce.

Sauces for Fish

For fish, a rich white sauce should be made from half fish stock and half milk – a meaty or bone stock would not give the correct flavour. The stock can be made up to the correct measure with the strained liquor left from cooking the fish when it is baked, grilled or steamed.

Fish Stock

you will need:

12 oz. to 1 lb. fish bones	*bouquet garni* (see page 19)
1 pint water	2 teaspoons salt
1 small chopped carrot and onion	2-inch strip lemon rind
1 chopped outer stalk celery	

1 Wash bones well; put in pan with water, prepared vegetables and seasonings.
2 Bring to boil, skim and simmer for 30 minutes without lid on pan. Strain, cool, and keep in covered container in fridge.
(Fish bones can usually be obtained from fishmonger, in addition to those removed from your own filleted fish.)

Rich White Sauce for Fish

you will need:

$\frac{1}{4}$ pint fish stock	1 oz. sieved flour
$\frac{1}{4}$ pint milk	$\frac{1}{4}$ teaspoon salt
1 oz. butter or margarine	good dash white pepper
	1 tablespoon top of milk

1 Warm milk and stock together. In another pan melt the butter, stir in flour gradually, adding a little warmed milk to prevent lumps, until smooth paste is formed.
2 Remove from heat, add remaining liquid slowly, beat well until smooth. Cook and stir 2–3 minutes, add seasonings, and cream with pan off heat.

For Cider Sauce: Add a tablespoon dry cider to $\frac{1}{2}$ pint White Sauce.

For Lemon Sauce: Add a dessertspoon lemon juice and $\frac{1}{2}$ teaspoon grated lemon rind to $\frac{1}{2}$ pint White Sauce.

For Parsley Sauce: Add a dessertspoon chopped parsley to $\frac{1}{2}$ pint White Sauce.

For Tomato Sauce: Add 2 tablespoons tomato purée to $\frac{1}{2}$ pint White Sauce.

For Cheese Sauce: Add 2–3 oz. grated dry Cheddar cheese to $\frac{1}{2}$ pint White Sauce.

For Egg Sauce: Add 1 finely chopped hard-boiled egg to $\frac{1}{2}$ pint White Sauce.

For Anchovy Sauce: Add 1 teaspoon anchovy essence or two pounded tinned anchovy fillets to 1 pint White Sauce; omit salt when making the White Sauce.

For Mustard Sauce: Add 2 teaspoons mustard mixed to a paste with white vinegar to $\frac{1}{2}$ pint White Sauce.

Baked Fillets; Cheese Sauce

you will need:

4 medium sized fillets cod or haddock	3 or 4 chopped chives or spring onions
salt and pepper	2 oz. butter or margarine
juice of $\frac{1}{2}$ lemon	$\frac{1}{4}$ to $\frac{1}{2}$ pint milk
	Cheese Sauce

1 Wipe the fillets, sprinkle with salt and pepper, squeeze lemon juice over cut sides.
2 Fold the fillets in halves lengthwise, cutting skin side lightly at the bend so they lie flat. (Folding prevents lemon juice coming in contact with milk and souring it.)
3 Put in a buttered casserole, side by side, sprinkle chopped chives or spring onions over; dot with butter or margarine.
4 Pour in milk to almost cover the fish; put lid or aluminium foil on casserole. Bake in moderate oven (355°F.—Gas Mark 4) 30–35 minutes.
5 Serve from the casserole, but pour off the liquor to add to stock for making Cheese Sauce (see this page).
Cutlets of Cod or Haddock can be baked in the same way; they should be about 1 inch thick. Keep the bone in, as it improves flavour.

Haddock Stuffed and Baked Whole

you will need:

1 medium sized whole haddock, 2–2$\frac{1}{2}$ lb.	good squeeze lemon juice
veal forcemeat (see page 34)	1 medium onion, sliced
salt and pepper	2 oz. butter or margarine

1 The under-side of the fish should be cut with scissors and the inside removed. Keep on the head, as it improves the flavour. Rinse well under running cold water; rub inside with salt to remove any blood or dark membranes.

2 Stuff the cavity of the haddock with the force-meat; sew up with coarse thread or fine string, leaving two loose ends so it can be pulled out after cooking.
3 Place in shallow cooking dish, buttered. Sprinkle with salt and pepper and lemon juice.
4 Arrange sliced onion down centre of fish; dot with butter or margarine and put remainder in bottom of cooking dish.
5 Cover and bake in moderate oven (355°F.—Gas Mark 4) for 30 to 40 minutes. Serve with Mustard or Lemon Sauce (see page 14).

Cutlets of Cod or **Haddock** can be stuffed and baked by removing the centre bone and filling the cavity with stuffing; they will take less time than whole fish – 25 to 30 minutes. Any surplus stuffing can be made into Force-meat Balls and baked in the dish alongside the fish.

Gurnet can be stuffed and baked using the same forcemeat; it is often covered with slices of streaky bacon as it is apt to cook dry. Serve with Anchovy or Parsley Sauce (see page 14).

For Baked Sea Bream do not attempt to remove the scales. Wash fish well after removing inside; make 3 or 4 slanting cuts right through the skin of the fish with a sharp pointed knife; put butter or margarine in these gashes after fish has been stuffed. Bake 40 to 45 minutes. When done, take up fish and with sharp pointed knife lift off the skin and scales which will come away together easily. Sprinkle fish with chopped parsley and serve with cut lemon and Parsley Sauce (see page 14).

Baked Mackerel: Head and tail fish, remove inside, stuff and sew up as for Baked Haddock, sprinkle with salt and pepper and a little flour. Bake with pieces of butter on top and in bottom of dish, and buttered paper or aluminium foil placed lightly on top. Serve with cut lemon and Cider Sauce (see page 14).

Haddock Rolls

you will need:

4 fillets fresh haddock	¼ teaspoon mixed herbs
4 chopped shallots, or pickling onions	salt and pepper
	little milk
2 oz. butter or margarine	tomatoes
3 tablespoons dry white breadcrumbs	

1 Wash and dry fillets; cut them down the centre, making 8 strips, about 1½ inches wide.
2 Mix shallots, butter or margarine, bread-crumbs, herbs, salt and pepper, and bind stiffly with a little milk. Spread each fillet with a little of the mixture.
3 Roll fillets up from the tail ends, stand them upright in a buttered baking dish, standing them close together so they stay upright.
4 Dot each fillet with a little extra butter, and pour in about ½ inch depth of milk.
5 Put quartered tomatoes around edge of dish; bake in moderate oven (355°F.—Gas Mark 4) 25 to 30 minutes. Serve with peas and carrots and Tomato Sauce (see page 14). If liked, the fillets can be spread with Veal Forcemeat (see page 34).

Cod Fillets in Cheese Batter

you will need:

4 tail-end fillets of cod	¼ teaspoon salt
2 oz. butter or margarine	dash of pepper
juice of ½ lemon	

For the batter:

4 oz. plain flour	½ pint milk and water (half and half)
¼ teaspoon salt	
1 egg	3 oz. finely grated dry cheese

1 Wash and dry fish. Butter a 3-inch deep fire-proof dish or Yorkshire pudding tin. Place fillets skin sides downwards in dish.
2 Melt remaining butter and pour over them. Squeeze lemon juice over them; sprinkle with salt and pepper.
3 Bake in hot oven (435°F.—Gas Mark 7) for 15 minutes.
4 Make the batter. Sieve flour and salt into mixing bowl, make well in centre and break egg into it.
5 Stir in egg, add half liquid and stir until smooth. Slowly add rest of liquid until smoothly blended, then beat 3–4 minutes.
6 Add cheese and beat for a minute or so longer.
7 When fish has baked for 15 minutes pour batter evenly over it. Bake 20 minutes longer, until batter is well risen and brown. Serve from dish, cut in squares.

Haddock and Mackerel Fillets may be cooked in the same way.

Scalloped Cod

you will need:

1½ lb. cod fillet	1 tablespoon capers
salt and pepper	8 oz. mushrooms
3 oz. butter	2 hard-boiled eggs
¼ pint milk	2 slices white toast
juice of ½ lemon	

1 Rinse the fish, poach it gently in water to just cover, with salt and pepper added, until it flakes easily.
2 Drain fish well, then flake, removing skin and bones, if any; stir in 1 oz. of the butter.
3 Heat the milk; add it to the fish. Season with lemon juice, and stir in the capers. Keep hot.
4 Heat remaining butter in pan and fry the mushrooms, adding a little salt and pepper.
5 Reserve a few of the best mushrooms for garnish; put remainder in a baking dish. Put fish mixture on top.
6 Garnish with sliced hard-boiled egg down centre of dish. Cut the toast into 8 triangles and stand them round the edge of the dish.
Haddock fillets may be used similarly.

Casserole of Cod

you will need:

4 cod cutlets or fillets (1½–2 lb.)	salt and pepper
8 oz. tomatoes	1 lb. potatoes
fat for frying	2 oz. dripping
2 or 3 sliced carrots	¼ pint milk or fish stock
1 large sliced onion	chopped parsley for garnish
1 chopped celery stalk	

1 Wash fish, removing fins; skin tomatoes and slice them.
2 Fry the carrots, onion and celery lightly in frying pan; remove them.
3 Put a layer of the sliced tomatoes in bottom of greased casserole, add the fried vegetables. Sprinkle with salt and pepper.
4 Pack the fish on top and cover with remaining tomatoes; sprinkle with salt and pepper.
5 Cover the whole with peeled and thinly sliced potatoes; put dripping in small dabs over the top. Pour in milk or stock.
6 Cover dish and cook in fairly hot oven (400°F. —Gas Mark 6) 45 minutes to 1 hour, removing lid for last 15 minutes to allow potatoes to brown. Sprinkle with chopped parsley when ready to serve.

Haddock may be cooked in the same way.

Fish Chowder (American Fish Stew)

you will need:

1½ lb. potatoes	1½ to 2 lb. cod or haddock fillets
2 oz. fat salt pork or bacon	salt and pepper
8 oz. onions, sliced	½ pint measure cracker crumbs or raspings
½ teaspoon curry powder	
¾ pint milk	

1 Boil potatoes in salted water to just cover, mash them and return them to the water in which they were boiled (there should be ½ pint water).
2 Cut fat pork or bacon into dice, fry it, add onions, cook until onions are transparent, stir in curry powder, add the milk.
3 Cut fish into neat pieces, removing skin and any bones: combine fish and potato mixture.
4 Add them to bacon and onion mixture in pan: cook gently 25 to 30 minutes. Season with salt and pepper.
5 Thicken with the cracker crumbs or raspings and serve very hot.

Baked Mackerel; Gooseberry Sauce

you will need:

2 medium sized mackerel, filleted	½ pint measure fine breadcrumbs
2 oz. butter or best margarine	lemon juice
	salt and pepper

For the sauce:

10 oz. can gooseberries, or 8 oz. fresh gooseberries or small jar bottled gooseberries	1 teaspoon cornflour
	little sugar, if necessary
	few drops green vegetable colouring

1 Wipe the fillets, cut them in halves across. Place in well buttered shallow ovenware dish.
2 Melt the butter in a saucepan, add the crumbs and stir until butter is absorbed.
3 Sprinkle lemon juice, salt and pepper over fish, then spread the buttered crumbs evenly over.
4 Cover with buttered paper and aluminium foil: bake in hot oven (400°F.—Gas Mark 6) 30 to 40 minutes. Serve from the baking dish.

To make Sauce:

1 Heat gooseberries in their juice if canned or bottled: if fresh, stew in a little water, adding sugar.
2 Rub through a sieve: return juice and pulp to pan to re-boil.

3 Blend cornflour to smooth paste with a little juice; add to pan when contents boil; stir until boiling and slightly thickened.

4 Add a few drops colouring to make a good green. Serve in sauce-boat.

This sauce may also be served with **Grilled Mackerel** or **Herrings**; the sharpness counteracts the oiliness of the fish.

Soused Herrings

you will need:

6 large herrings	1 teaspoon mixed
6 slices onion	pickling spice
½ teaspoon salt	malt vinegar to cover
6 bay leaves	little water

1 Have the herrings boned; place a slice of onion on the flesh side of each; sprinkle with salt.

2 Roll up from the tail ends; pack closely in baking dish so they will not unroll.

3 Put a bay leaf between each fish and sprinkle the pickling spice over them.

4 Mix vinegar with a quarter as much water and pour over the fish.

5 Bake in a fairly hot oven (400°F.—Gas Mark 6) for 30–35 minutes.

The roes may be cooked with the fish. Can be eaten hot or cold, but are better flavoured when cold.

Mackerel can be soused in the same way, but will take a little longer cooking.

Both **Herring** and **Mackerel** can be soused whole, when the onion rings should be arranged on top of the fish.

Baked Haddock with Parsley Sauce *(see back cover)*

you will need:

4 haddock fillets	1 oz. butter
1 teaspoon lemon juice	slices of lemon for garnish
salt and pepper	

For Parsley Sauce:

½ large can (6½ fl. oz.) evaporated milk	salt and pepper
2 oz. flour	2 tablespoons finely chopped parsley
2 oz. butter	

1 Roll up the haddock fillets from head to tail and place in a greased casserole. Sprinkle with lemon juice, salt and pepper, and dot with butter.

2 Cover with a piece of buttered greaseproof paper, and bake in a moderate oven (350°F—Gas Mark 4) for 20 minutes until tender.

3 Meanwhile, make the evaporated milk up to 1 pint with water and whisk in the flour.

4 Place in a saucepan with the butter and stir over a moderate heat until the sauce boils and thickens. Continue to cook, stirring, for 3–4 minutes.

5 Season to taste with salt and pepper, and stir in the parsley.

6 Serve at once with the baked fish, garnished with slices of lemon.

How to Buy and Cook Meat

Beef

Beef is the favourite and most useful meat for the housewife who has to make good and appetising meals on a low budget. Leaving aside the most expensive cuts – sirloin, ribs, and the grilling cuts: rump and fillet – there are still a number of inexpensive cuts that can be pot-roasted, made into stews or casseroled, or used to make puddings, pies and curries.

Prime beef is a deep cherry red in the lean, marbled with fat, with a firm, elastic texture. Fat should be creamy coloured though this can vary to a clearish yellow according to the breed and diet of the ox. Avoid rosy-pink beef; it is a sign that the meat has not been well hung, is too newly-killed, and will be lacking in flavour. The most expensive joints, such as sirloin, wing rib or long rib are best roasted at a high temperature (450° to 500°F.—Gas Mark 7–8). The less expensive joints such as top-side, top-rump, silverside, brisket, are best slow roasted in a covered tin, or pot-roasted, or boiled with vegetables.

Among the less expensive cuts are:

Top-Side – A very lean cut; a piece of fat is usually skewered to one side so it will not cook dry. There is no bone. Can be slow roasted or pot-roasted.

Top-Rump – Similar to top-side, but has its own fat. For slow roasting, but better braised or pot-roasted.

Silverside – For the traditional boiled beef and carrots. Lean, with a nut of fat at the side. It can be bought fresh, but for boiling is better salted. Most butchers keep silverside ready salted. To avoid over-saltiness it should be soaked an hour or so in cold water before cooking. It is the favourite cold meat for sandwiches, or served with salad.

Brisket – Best pot-roasted and eaten cold; sometimes it is salted or spiced. Used also for pressed beef; in which case it is best to use two pieces, and after cooking place them on top of each other and press in an oblong loaf tin.

Chuck and **Blade-Bone Steak** – For meat puddings, slow casseroling, or pies. For pies it should be pre-cooked and left to go cold.

Flank – The cheapest cut of beef, rather fatty. It is a good eker-out of lean beef in pies and puddings. It can be pickled and salted and pressed when excess fat is removed.

Buttock Steak – You will probably get this if you just ask for 'stewing steak'. Good for steak and kidney pudding as it requires long, slow cooking, but it is well flavoured coming from near the rump.

Shin or **Leg** – An excellent cheap cut; lean, but run through with gristle which will soften and enrich the gravy in long, slow cooking. It can be used in stewed steak with ox kidney, or in pies after pre-cooking. Excellent for beef bouillon or strong beef soup.

Neck and **Clod** – Often known as Soup Meat; use for stewing or in puddings. Frequently included in ready-minced beef. (It's best to buy buttock or chuck steak and ask the butcher to mince it for you.)

Other Parts of beef are the **Offal** – Heart, liver, kidney, tripe, cow-heel, sweetbreads, tongue, oxtail, ox cheek, suet.

Recipes

Slow Oven-roast Beef

you will need:

3–4 oz. dripping
$2\frac{1}{2}$ or 3 lb. either top-side, top-rump, brisket, or unsalted silverside beef
salt and pepper

1 Pre-heat oven to 375°F.—Gas Mark 5.
2 Heat half the dripping in roasting tin on top of stove ring.
3 Wipe the meat, sprinkle with salt and pepper.
4 Place in the hot dripping in roasting tin for 1 minute; turn and sear meat on second side; this seals in the juices that would escape if meat was put straight into slow oven.
5 Put meat on a rack or trivet in tin; baste well with hot dripping.
6 If self-basting roasting tin is used cover meat with lid; if not cover with foil.
7 Put tin in centre of oven and roast, allowing 25 to 30 minutes per lb. according to thickness. Turn meat half-way through roasting.
8 Remove lid or foil 30 minutes before meat is done to allow outside to brown. Serve with clear gravy.

To make Gravy:

1 Remove meat from tin on to hot dish, pour off fat in tin, leaving behind the brown sediment. Sprinkle this with salt and pepper, then stir in $\frac{1}{2}$ pint stock or water with bouillon cube added.
2 Place tin over low boiling ring, and heat mixture until boiling, stirring well to blend in the brown sediment. Pour into hot gravy boat.

Pot-Roast Beef

you will need:

3 lb. of any of the joints given for slow roasting
little flour
salt and pepper
3–4 oz. dripping
1 medium sized onion or 4 shallots
$\frac{1}{4}$ pint water or stock

1 Wipe the meat and rub flour, salt and pepper well into all sides of it.
2 Heat the dripping in a heavy saucepan or flame-proof casserole; brown the meat all over in the hot dripping.
3 Add the sliced onion or the shallots, whole.
4 Add the water, put close-fitting lid on pan or casserole.

5 Reduce heat and simmer until tender allowing 30 to 35 minutes to the lb.

If pot-roast is to be eaten hot, a few root vegetables may be added during last hour of cooking, to serve separately.

If liked, meat can be pot-roasted in slow oven (350°F.—Gas Mark 4).

Braised Beef

Same joints of beef are used, with carrots, onions, celery, turnips added.

1 Brown meat in hot dripping on all sides.
2 Take up the meat; brown the prepared, cut up vegetables in the same fat.
3 Put bed of vegetables in stew-jar, add salt and a sprinkling of herbs. Put meat on top, pour in stock or water to cover vegetables only.
4 Cover tightly and cook slowly on top of stove or in oven, allowing 40 to 50 minutes to the lb.

Boiled Silverside, Carrots and Dumplings

you will need:

3½ to 4 lb. salt silverside	pepper
12 oz. to 1 lb. carrots	2 bay leaves
8 oz. small onions	

1 Soak meat at least an hour: take up and wipe dry.
2 Put into saucepan or flame-proof casserole with water to cover. Bring to boiling point, remove scum and simmer 30 minutes.
3 Add carrots, scraped and cut into equal sizes, and the onions, whole, the pepper and bay leaf. Cover closely and simmer for 1 hour longer.
4 Add the dumplings and boil gently for further 20 to 30 minutes.
5 Dish up with carrots and dumplings round the meat and use cooking liquor for gravy.

For the Dumplings:

4 oz. flour	½ teaspoon salt
2 oz. shredded suet	water
1 level teaspoon baking powder	

1 Mix all the dry ingredients.
2 Add water gradually to make a pliable dough.
3 Form into small balls on a floured board, and drop them into fast-boiling meat liquor. Reduce heat and boil gently until done. (Dumplings will rise to the top when done.)

Self-raising flour may be used, omitting baking powder.

Spiced Brisket of Beef

you will need:

3½ to 4 lb. boned and rolled brisket of beef	2 pickled walnuts
	½ pint stock or water
2 slices collar bacon	salt and pepper
bouquet garni (sprig parsley and thyme, bay leaf, blade mace, 6 peppercorns, tied up in muslin)	1 onion
	2 small carrots
	level tablespoon flour
	½ tablespoon bottled spicy sauce
6 cloves	
¼ teaspoon whole allspice	

1 Wipe the meat; put one slice bacon in bottom of a stewpan, put in the meat, and lay second slice of bacon on top.
2 Add the *bouquet garni*, cloves, allspice and chopped pickled walnuts.
3 Pour in the stock or water, sprinkle with salt and pepper and cook gently for 2 hours.
4 Dice onion and carrots and add to the pan, and continue cooking until meat is tender – another 1 to 1½ hours.
5 Take up the meat on to a hot dish. Remove *bouquet garni* from liquor in pan.
6 Mix flour to a smooth paste with a little of the liquor and add the bottled spicy sauce.
7 Boil up the liquor in pan, stir in the blended flour and sauce; bring to the boil again and simmer 2–3 minutes. Pour into sauce-boat.

Beef Rolls or Olives

you will need:

1½ lb. lean beef	level tablespoon flour
salt and pepper	¾ pint stock or dissolved bouillon cube
4 oz. forcemeat (page 20)	
2 oz. dripping	½ tablespoon mushroom ketchup or pickled walnut vinegar
1 small onion	
1 outside stick celery	
	3 cloves

1 Cut the meat into neat, thin slices, about 4 inches square. Sprinkle with salt and pepper. Spread forcemeat on each square, roll and tie or skewer securely.
2 Heat dripping in thick saucepan, and fry the beef rolls until lightly browned all over. Take up and keep hot.
3 Chop vegetables and fry lightly in fat in pan; add flour and stir until smooth and lightly browned. Pour in stock and ketchup and add cloves; bring to the boil.
4 Return the beef rolls to the pan, cover with greased paper and tight-fitting lid and simmer 1½ to 1¾ hours.
5 Take up the beef rolls, remove ties or skewers, and arrange on hot dish. Season sauce again if necessary, strain it and pour over the rolls. Pipe or fork up a border of mashed potatoes around the dish.

For the Forcemeat:

3 tablespoons breadcrumbs
1 tablespoon shredded suet
level teaspoon mixed
  herbs
pepper and salt
1 small egg or a little
  milk

Mix breadcrumbs, suet and herbs, season with salt and pepper. Bind stiffly with beaten egg or a little milk.

Haricot Oxtail

you will need:

1 oxtail, jointed
8 oz. onions
2 cloves
bouquet garni (see
  page 19)
8 oz. carrots
1 small turnip
6 oz. cooked haricot beans
1–1½ oz. flour
1 teaspoon chopped
  parsley
salt and pepper

1 Remove surplus fat from oxtail and wash. Stick one onion with cloves.
2 Put oxtail in saucepan, with onion stuck with cloves, *bouquet garni* and water to well cover. Simmer 1 hour.
3 Strain off gravy, allow to go cold then skim off as much fat as possible. Return gravy to pan with the oxtail; bring to the boil.
4 Add remaining vegetables cut in strips: simmer until vegetables are tender, then add haricot beans; simmer for 30 minutes.
5 Thicken gravy with blended flour; add chopped parsley, season with salt and pepper. Simmer 3 minutes after adding blended flour, then pour all into a hot dish.

Savoury Mince

you will need:

1 large onion
1 oz. dripping
12 oz. minced chuck or
  buttock steak
level tablespoon flour
½ pint stock or dissolved
  bouillon cube
salt and pepper
1 teaspoon Worcester-
  shire sauce
triangles of toast

1 Peel onion and chop finely. Melt dripping and fry onion in it until golden brown.
2 Put in the minced steak, stir well with fork and cook for 5 minutes.
3 Sprinkle flour over the meat and mix well; add stock gradually, stirring over low heat until boiling point is reached.
4 Add salt and pepper, and Worcestershire sauce and simmer 45 minutes to 1 hour, stirring from time to time.
5 Serve in a hot shallow dish, garnished with triangles of toast arranged around edge of dish.

Hamburgers

you will need:

12 oz. minced chuck or
  buttock steak
4 oz. coarse oatmeal or
  fine breadcrumbs
¼ teaspoon mixed herbs
1 level tablespoon onion,
  finely chopped or grated
2 teaspoons Worcester-
  shire sauce
1 beaten egg
little stock (about 1
  tablespoon)
1 level teaspoon salt
¼ teaspoon pepper
¼ teaspoon mustard
  powder
little flour
fat for frying

1 Mix the minced meat with the oatmeal and mixed herbs. Add the grated onion, and mix thoroughly.
2 Stir in the beaten egg, Worcestershire sauce and sufficient stock to make a stiff mixture.
3 Add salt and pepper and mustard; mix well.
4 Turn the mixture on to a floured board: divide into eight portions and shape into rounds.
5 Fry in shallow fat for 15 minutes, or until cooked in the centre, turning often. Put a lid over the pan during frying to conserve heat.
6 Serve between split soft rolls, or with mashed potatoes if preferred.

Braised Ox liver

you will need:

8 oz. ox liver, sliced
1 heaped tablespoon flour
2 oz. dripping or cooking
  fat
1 medium sized chopped
  onion
2 rashers bacon, chopped
2 medium sized carrots,
  sliced
2 outer stalks celery,
  chopped
salt and pepper
pinch mixed herbs
½ pint stock or water

1 Remove skin, pipes and gristle from liver: soak liver in cold water with a little salt added, for 1 hour. Strain and dry liver.
2 Flour the liver; fry in the hot fat with the onion and bacon until brown on both sides.
3 Remove liver from pan and toss the remaining vegetables in the fat, 2–3 minutes. Replace the liver, add salt and pepper and herbs.
4 Pour in the stock or water, bring to the boil, cover closely and simmer on top of stove or in oven 1½ to 1¾ hours.
5 Add remaining flour, mixed to a smooth paste with stock or water, simmer 2–3 minutes to cook the flour; dish up on to hot dish and serve with extra vegetables.

Beef Heart

This can be sliced and braised in the same way as liver, after all tubes and gristle have been removed, and the slices soaked in salt water for an hour.

Heart and Kidney Pie

you will need:

1 sheep's heart	½ pint water or stock
8 oz. ox kidney, or	little meat or vegetable
2 sheep's kidneys	extract
1 medium onion, chopped	2 medium sized potatoes
½ teaspoon mixed herbs	8 oz. short pastry
salt and pepper	(see page 64)

1 Remove excess fat and tubes from heart: skin kidney and remove core.
2 Soak heart and kidney in salted water for 1 hour, then drain and cut into small pieces.
3 Put into saucepan with chopped onion, herbs, salt and pepper, add water or stock and meat or vegetable extract.
4 Simmer 30 or 40 minutes, stirring often.
5 Slice the potatoes thinly.
6 Put meat, etc., into pie dish, cover with sliced potato then with pastry lid.
7 Mark edges with fork: decorate with pastry leaves.
8 Make a hole in top of pastry for steam to escape: bake in hot oven (425°F.—Gas Mark 7), 20 to 25 minutes, until pastry is a good brown.

Sausages Sweet and Sour

you will need:

8 skinless sausages	¼ teaspoon grated horse-
2 tablespoons corn oil	radish, or horseradish
1 large onion, sliced	sauce
1 green pepper, seeded	1 tablespoon chopped sweet
and sliced	pickle or chutney
1 small can sliced pineapple	1 large tomato, cut in
1 tablespoon cornflour	eighths
1 bouillon cube	hot cooked rice
1 teaspoon Worcestershire	
sauce	

1 Cut sausages in pieces 2 inches long; brown in oil in frying pan. Stir in the onion, sliced seeded pepper and cook 2 minutes.
2 Drain pineapple; cut slices into quarters. Measure pineapple juice and add water to make up to ½ pint.
3 Blend cornflour to smooth paste with a little water, add to the juice and water, add crushed bouillon cube; stir until dissolved.
4 Stir in the Worcestershire sauce, pineapple, pickle, horseradish and tomato. Add to the sausages.
5 Cook slowly over low heat for 10 minutes, stirring occasionally. Serve on bed of hot rice.

Farmhouse Sausage Pie

you will need:

1 oz. butter or margarine	1 teaspoon chopped parsley
8 oz. onions, finely sliced	8 oz. short pastry (see
1 lb. potatoes, peeled and	page 64)
sliced	milk to glaze
1½ lb. beef sausages	
¾ pint cider and water	
mixed	

1 Melt butter or margarine in medium-sized saucepan, and fry and stir the onions and potatoes in it for 10 minutes.
2 Turn into a 2-pint ovenware dish. Cut sausages into thirds and stir in.
3 Add cider and water and sprinkle with chopped parsley.
4 Roll out pastry, dampen edges of dish, and cover with pastry. Mark the edges with a fork, and prick with fork to allow steam to escape. Decorate top with pastry leaves.
5 Brush over with milk. Bake in hot oven (445°F. —Gas Mark 8) for 10 minutes, then lower heat to moderate (350°F.—Gas Mark 4) and bake for a further 40 to 50 minutes.

Lamb and Mutton

The joints of lamb and mutton are identical; you can tell which is which by the size of the joints and the colour. Lamb, being younger has smaller joints: the flesh is rosy pink with practically no grain to it, and the fat is almost pure white and very firm. Mutton is darker and coarser, the cuts are larger, and there is much more fat than there is on lamb.

Even the most expensive cuts of lamb or mutton are considerably cheaper than beef, but when it is in season there is nothing to beat English lamb for flavour and tenderness. Imported frozen lamb and mutton are very good too, and if it has been carefully de-frosted and well hung by the butcher and roasted in not too hot an oven, is as tender and juicy as English. There is less fat on the imported frozen lamb, too.

Leg of lamb or mutton, and the loin are the most expensive roasting joints. The leg is a rather large joint, even in lamb, weighing 4½ to 5½ lb. It is usually cut in half, making the Fillet end, and the Shank end. Both joints are suitable for roasting: the Fillet end has very little bone. Shank end has more bone and is therefore a little cheaper but the meat is more tender than the expensive Fillet end, and there is very little fat. Lamb chops are cut from the loin and are expensive, though to my mind they are no more flavoursome or tender than the cheaper Best End of Neck cutlets, and they are certainly fatter.

Roasting Lamb or Mutton

The meat should be well cooked, but not dried up. Allow 20 minutes to the lb. and 20 minutes over, but allowance must be made for the thickness of the joint: a thin joint like Best End of Neck will probably not require the extra 20 minutes. Stuffed joints take longer, usually an extra 5 minutes to the lb.

The inexpensive cuts of lamb and mutton are:

Shoulder – Fatter than the leg, with more bone, but a more tender, sweeter meat. It is often boned and stuffed. The butcher will bone it, but don't have it rolled and tied if you want to stuff it.

Best End of Neck – Most often used as cutlets but makes a good roast. The meat should be chined (thick back-bone sawn through), by the butcher, the skin removed, and the end bones cracked 3–4 inches from the ends, so that the thin end can be folded under the joint in roasting tin.

Chump Chops – Cut from the end of loin nearest the leg, or from the fillet end of the leg itself. Can be grilled, but better oven-fried with tomatoes and onions.

Middle End Neck – Comes next to Best End. Use for stews and hot-pots: it should be well chopped and surplus fat removed. It is also used for Scotch broth.

Scrag End Neck – Comes next to Middle End Neck. Used chiefly for stews and hot-pots. Lean meat is excellent and very cheap for mutton pies, and the bones for soup. Gristle in neck gives richness to gravy after slow cooking.

Breast – Very cheap. Often boned, stuffed, rolled and roasted. It can be stewed but is rather fat. A good way is to stew it: leave it to go cold with a weight on top: then remove bones, cut meat into slices removing excess fat, then fry meat.

Offal – Heart, Liver, Kidneys, Head and Tongue.

Boned Roast Stuffed Shoulder of Lamb (see front cover)

you will need:

1 oz. cooking fat or dripping	½ teaspoon parsley, chopped or dried
1 tablespoon chopped onion	½ teaspoon mixed herbs
4 good tablespoons fresh white breadcrumbs	1 tablespoon chopped fresh mint
salt and pepper	1–2 tablespoons milk
	1 boned shoulder of lamb

1 Melt fat in a small saucepan and gently fry the onion for 1 minute.
2 Add breadcrumbs, salt and pepper, herbs and mint and mix stiffly with milk.
3 Spread over the lamb, roll up and tie securely with fine string.
4 Place in a roasting tin with a little dripping to start the roasting and cook in a moderate oven (350°F.—Gas Mark 4) allowing 30 minutes to the lb.

Stuffed Breast of Lamb or Mutton

you will need:

1 good sized breast of lamb or mutton (1½ to 2 lb.), boned	forcemeat
	salt and pepper
	1 tablespoon flour

1 Spread the boned meat out flat: remove surplus fat from inside.
2 Work the stuffing well into the spaces left from boning: spread any surplus evenly over the meat.
3 Roll up the narrow way of the breast, and tie securely.
4 Place in roasting tin with pieces of fat cut from meat. Roast in hot oven (425°F.—Gas Mark 7) allowing 20 minutes to the lb. and 20 minutes over.
5 Fifteen minutes before end of cooking, baste the meat well, sprinkle with salt and pepper and half the flour. Baste again and return meat to oven to crisp and brown outside.
Serve with thick brown gravy.

For the Forcemeat:

½ pint dry white breadcrumbs	1 tablespoon chopped onion
1 teaspoon mixed herbs	¼ teaspoon salt
2 teaspoons chopped parsley	good pinch black pepper
	egg, milk or stock to bind

Mix all these ingredients well and bind stiffly with egg, milk or stock. (As the meat is fatty, no fat is added to forcemeat.)

For the gravy: After removing meat to hot dish, pour off fat from roasting tin, retaining 1 tablespoon of fat in tin. Sprinkle in remaining flour, season with salt and pepper and stir over low heat until flour is well blended with fat and sediment and is a good brown. Stir in slowly ½ pint stock or water, stir until boiling. Simmer 1–2 minutes; pour into gravy boat.

Boiled Lamb or Mutton; Caper Sauce

you will need:

Shank end leg of lamb or mutton (2½ to 3 lb.)	medium sized turnip, quartered
salt and pepper	outer stalk celery
good pinch dried mint, or sprig of fresh mint	medium sized onion
4 small carrots	caper sauce

1 Ask the butcher to chop the shank bone, without severing it. Put meat in large saucepan, add salt and pepper and mint.
2 Cover with water or stock; bring to the boil; skim. Put on tight-fitting lid, and cook just below boiling point allowing 20 minutes to the lb. and 20 minutes over.
3 45 minutes before meat is done, add the prepared vegetables and complete cooking.
4 Take up meat on to hot dish and put vegetables around it. Serve caper sauce separately; a little of the stock from boiling meat is served as gravy.

For the Caper Sauce:

1 oz. butter or best margarine	salt and pepper
1 oz. sieved flour	1 tablespoon chopped capers
½ pint milk and stock mixed (half of each)	

Melt butter or margarine, add flour away from heat and stir until blended. Add enough milk and stock to make a smooth paste. Return pan to low heat and add rest of liquid gradually, beating well. Stir until boiling, cook for 2 minutes. Add seasoning and capers, stir until boiling again and pour into sauce-boat.

For **Haricot Lamb** or **Mutton** add 6 oz. haricot beans, soaked overnight, at the same time as the vegetables.

Summer Lamb Stew

you will need:

1½ lb. middle neck lamb	8–10 spring onions
salt and pepper	12 oz. new potatoes
8 oz. young carrots	1 lb. shelled garden peas
2 small young turnips, quartered	1 teaspoon chopped mint

1 Joint the meat (butcher will do this), wash it, and put into pan with salt and pepper and hot water to cover.
2 Bring to the boil and simmer 20 minutes. Add the carrots, turnips and onions (green parts as well).
3 Simmer 10 minutes, then add potatoes (small and even sized).
4 Simmer 10 minutes, then add the peas and chopped mint and simmer 15 minutes. Serve meat and vegetables on hot dish; sprinkle extra chopped mint over.

Lamb Hot-Pot
(see back cover)

you will need:

2 lb. neck of lamb	1 lb. potatoes
1 oz. dripping	½ pint stock
2 onions	chopped parsley or sprig of parsley
1 teaspoon mixed herbs	
salt and pepper	

1 Prepare, trim and cut the neck into pieces. Fry the meat in the dripping in a pan.
2 Remove the meat and lightly fry the sliced onions.
3 Place a layer of meat, then a little of the onion and a sprinkling of the herbs and seasoning in a casserole. Then cover with a layer of potato. Repeat this process until all the ingredients have been used, finishing with a layer of potato.
4 Pour in the stock, cover with a lid and cook in a moderately hot oven (375°F.—Gas Mark 5), for about 2 hours.
5 30 minutes before the end of the cooking time remove the lid to allow the potatoes to brown. Sprinkle chopped parsley on top or decorate with a sprig of parsley, and serve from the casserole.

Stuffed Sheep's Hearts

you will need:

4 sheep or lambs' hearts	salt and pepper
6 oz. forcemeat	little flour

1 Using kitchen scissors cut off flaps, lobes and membranes from the hearts. Rinse and soak in salted water at least an hour.
2 Rinse hearts in running cold water: squeezing well to remove any blood.
3 Dry, and then fill cavities with the forcemeat, pressing it well in. Roll each in flour seasoned with salt and pepper.
4 Place in a shallow ovenware dish where they can lay side by side. Add a little dripping, and cover with greased paper or foil.
5 Bake in fairly hot oven (400°F.—Gas Mark 6) 1½ to 2 hours. Any surplus forcemeat should be rolled into balls on floured board and baked with the hearts.
6 Take up hearts and forcemeat balls on to hot dish, add a little water or stock (¼ to ½ pint) to sediment in dish, stir over low heat until boiling, and pour over the hearts. A little extra flour may be added if a thicker gravy is liked.

For the Forcemeat:

4 oz. brown or white breadcrumbs	½ teaspoon mixed herbs
2 oz. shredded suet	salt and pepper
2 teaspoons chopped parsley	milk, egg or stock to bind
rind of half lemon, grated	

Mix breadcrumbs and suet, add parsley, lemon rind and mixed herbs, a good pinch salt and sprinkling of pepper. Mix well: bind stiffly with milk, beaten egg or stock.

Sheep or Lambs' Liver with Stuffing

you will need:

8 oz. liver, sliced	4 rashers streaky bacon
6 oz. forcemeat, as for hearts	4 tablespoons stock or water

1 Wash liver well, remove any skin or tubes: soak liver 30 minutes in salted water.
2 Drain and rinse liver, dry it and lay it in greased ovenware dish.
3 Spread stuffing over each slice: cover with bacon, rinds removed.
4 Add stock or water: bake in fairly hot oven 30 to 45 minutes.
5 Serve from the baking dish, adding a little more boiling stock if first amount has evaporated.

Kidneys with Stuffing and Tomatoes

you will need:

4 sheep or lambs' kidneys	4 rashers bacon
6 oz. forcemeat, as for hearts	4 tomatoes

1 Split each kidney open lengthwise without quite dividing it (start from rounded side through to the core). Remove skin and cores.
2 Proceed as for liver, arranging quartered tomatoes around edge of dish.

Kidneys with Mushrooms

Substitute 4 oz. mushrooms for the tomatoes, or a mixture of tomatoes and mushrooms may be used.

Braised Sheep's Tongues

you will need:

4 sheep's tongues	*bouquet garni* (see page 19)
2 oz. best margarine	pepper and salt
1 carrot	½ pint stock
1 onion	2 slices streaky bacon
1 small turnip	½ pint rich brown sauce
outside stick of celery	

1 Remove pipes, surplus fat and skin from roots of tongues. Soak tongues in salted water 1–1½ hours.
2 Put in pan with cold water to cover, boil up, strain through a colander and rinse under running cold water. Dry them well.
3 Heat margarine in stewpan or saucepan, add chopped vegetables and toss over low heat until lightly browned all over.
4 Add *bouquet garni*, salt and pepper, arrange the tongues on top of vegetables, cover pan and simmer for 20 minutes. Add stock to nearly cover the bed of vegetables.
5 Put bacon, rinds removed, on top of tongues, cover with greased paper, then with lid, and simmer 2–2½ hours, until tender.
6 When done, take up tongues, skin them, split them down the middles lengthwise, put on a dish skinned sides uppermost and coat with thick brown sauce. Serve extra sauce in sauce-boat.

For the Brown Sauce:

1 oz. dripping	½ pint stock or dissolved bouillon cube
1 small onion	
1 oz. flour	small carrot
	¼ small turnip

Melt dripping, slice onion and fry until transparent. Add flour, stir until blended and cook slowly until brown. Stir in stock, away from heat, stir until boiling and skim well. Add vegetables and seasoning. Simmer 25 to 30 minutes, then strain.

Boiled Sheep's Tongues

After preparing the tongues as for Braised Tongues, put them in a pan with all the other ingredients (except Brown Sauce). Simmer for 1¼ to 1½ hours, until tender when tested in thickest part with fork. Take up, remove skins while hot, cut tongues in slices lengthwise, arrange on serving dish, coat with Brown Sauce. The streaky bacon may be chopped and added to the sauce. Extra vegetables may be boiled with the tongues and served separately.

Boiled Sheep's Head

you will need:

1 sheep's head, split and snout bones removed by butcher	2 onions, sliced
	2 carrots, sliced
	1 small turnip, sliced
bouquet garni (see page 19)	2 tablespoons pearl barley
salt and pepper	¾ pint white sauce

1 Remove the brains from the head; put them to soak in salted water. Wash head in several lots of warm water, then let it stand for an hour in salted water. Strain and rinse.
2 Put in large pan, cover with cold water, boil up, pour off water and cover again with cold water. Add bouquet garni, pepper and salt, boil up and skim. Simmer 1 hour.
3 Add sliced vegetables, the washed barley and simmer for a further 1½ hours.
4 Strain water from the brains, remove dark membranes; tie brains in muslin, add to pan and simmer 10 to 15 minutes. Take out and chop them coarsely.
5 Add the brains to ¾ pint white sauce, made as for Caper Sauce (see page 23) using liquor from boiling head for mixing.
6 When head is done, take up and cut meat from cheeks and neck. Skin and slice the tongue.
7 Arrange meat on a dish, pour the Brain Sauce over and garnish with slices of tongue and the vegetables. Re-season a little of the broth and serve as gravy.

Lamb Patties

you will need:

6 oz. short pastry (see page 64)	1 level teaspoon capers
	½ teaspoon made mustard
8 oz. cooked lamb, minced	salt and pepper
1 medium sized onion, chopped	a little gravy or stock

1 Roll out the pastry to line 4–6 patty tins, depending on size, reserving some for pastry lids.
2 Mix lamb, onion, capers, mustard, salt and pepper to taste, and moisten with a little gravy.
3 Divide this mixture between the lined patty tins; cover with pastry lids, squeezing edges well together.
4 Make hole in top of each; bake in fairly hot oven (400°F.—Gas Mark 6) for 20 to 25 minutes, until pastry is a good brown.
The meat mixture may be moistened with a little tomato sauce instead of gravy, and a slice of tomato placed on top of the meat before putting on pastry lid.

Pork and Bacon

Pork, on the whole, is by no means cheap, though the prime cuts are cheaper than the prime cuts of beef. It is apt to be rather fat, which makes it uneconomical as it shrinks a lot in cooking. Butchers have tried to get over the housewives' dislike of fat by cutting away a lot of the pork fat before selling it, thus making it more expensive (to make up for the loss in weight which they have to pay for) and depriving us of the crackling.

The lean of pork should be a pale pink and fine-grained, and the fat really white. The rind if left on, should be soft and a light flesh tint; tough, hard rind denotes an old pig and the meat will cook dry and tough – another reason why it is best to buy pork with the rind on; it shows whether you are buying old or young meat.

Pork should always be well cooked; under-cooked pork is not only unpalatable, but it is indigestible and a real danger to health. Allow 25 minutes to the lb. and 25 minutes over. It is not necessary to baste pork when roasting it; the scored rind should be exposed to dry heat to get good crisp crackling.

The loin and the leg are the prime cuts for roasting; the leg is often cut in two, the fillet end and shank end, as in the case of lamb.

Inexpensive cuts are:

Hand – The front legs, but just as tasty as leg. Inclined to be fatty, but is quite tender. It roasts well (25 minutes to the lb. and 25 over) but is perhaps better gently boiled with pease pudding; it also eats well cold.

Spare Ribs or Neck – Comes next to the loin: it can be roasted, but a more popular way is to chop it between the bones in chunky pieces and fry them. It is excellent for casseroles.

Blade Bone – A bony piece lying below the spare rib. It makes a good casserole; sometimes it is boned out, then stuffed, rolled and roasted.

Belly Pork – Often salted, boiled and pressed to be eaten cold, but it can be bought fresh and makes a tender roast if rather fat. The piece nearest the shoulder or hand is thicker and leaner than the leg end and more suitable for roasting.

Offal – Include trotters, head, kidneys, heart, liver. Pig's fry consists of the heart, liver, sweetbread, parts of the stomach, a little flesh or fat from the belly.

The 'trimmings' of pork are almost as important as the meat itself, and they serve a definite purpose. For instance, a bready forcemeat, or a pease pudding, balances the fat, while acid accompaniments such as apple sauce or a spicy one such as mustard sauce 'cut' the fat and aid digestion.

Roast Spare-Ribs or Neck of Pork

you will need:

2–2½ lb. pork	salt
6 oz. forcemeat as for Stuffed Sheep's Hearts (see page 24)	apple rings or apple sauce brown gravy (see page 23)
little dripping	

1 Have the pork boned by the butcher; simmer bones, with an onion for stock.
2 Press the forcemeat into the spaces left from boning; spread surplus smoothly over the meat, roll up and tie.
3 Place in roasting tin with a little dripping in the bottom; sprinkle rind of meat with salt.
4 Roast in hot oven (445°F.—Gas Mark 8) 25 minutes to the lb. and 25 minutes over.
5 Take up on to hot dish, pour off fat from tin and make thickened brown gravy (see page 23). If apple rings are served, arrange around meat; put apple sauce in sauce-boat.

Apple Rings or Sauce:

2 large cooking apples	½ tablespoon demerara sugar

For the Sauce:

1 tablespoon water	½ teaspoon butter

For the rings: core apples, wipe them, cut into ¼-inch slices. 30 minutes before meat is cooked put the rings in the hot dripping, sprinkle half sugar over. Cook 15 minutes, turn rings and sprinkle with remaining sugar. Cook 15 minutes longer or until apple rings are brown and sugar melted.

For Apple Sauce: Peel and core apples, cut in quarters then in slices. Put in pan with water and sugar; simmer until apples are soft, stirring from time to time. When apples are soft, beat them well, adding the butter during beating. Pour into sauce-boat.

Braised Spare-Ribs

you will need:

2 lb. spare-ribs, chopped into pieces	½ tablespoon flour
3 oz. pork dripping or margarine	¼ pint stock or water
1 medium sized chopped onion	2 teaspoons tomato purée or ketchup
1 chopped clove of garlic (if liked)	good pinch dried sage salt and pepper

1 Heat the dripping or margarine; brown pieces of pork in it on all sides. Remove the meat.
2 Add the onion and garlic and cook until beginning to turn brown in the same pan. Garlic may be omitted.
3 Stir in the flour; when smooth, add stock slowly stirring all the time.
4 Add the tomato purée, the sage and salt and pepper, stir until smooth, then bring to the boil.
5 Replace the pork, cover and cook over very low heat for 1 to 1½ hours, or cook in moderate oven (355°F.—Gas Mark 4) 1½ to 2 hours.

Stuffed and Rolled Belly Pork

Bone, stuff and roll, using same forcemeat stuffing as for Roast Spare-ribs (this page). Serve with Apple Sauce and thickened brown gravy (see page 23).

Hand of Pork

Bone, stuff and roll, and roast in same way.

Boiled Hand or Shoulder Pork: Pease Pudding

you will need:

3 lb. shoulder (or hand) pork	1 large onion
3 sage leaves or ¼ teaspoon dried sage	¼ medium turnip
3 medium carrots	2 or 3 stalks celery
	6 peppercorns

1 Put pork in large pan, cover with warm water, bring to boil.
2 Skim, boil for 15 minutes, then add sage, quartered carrots, sliced onion, turnip, chopped celery and peppercorns.
3 Boil steadily. Allow 20 minutes to the lb. An hour before meat is done add the pease pudding.

For the Pudding:

1 pint green split peas, soaked overnight	1 oz. margarine
sprig mint	1 egg
	salt and pepper

1 Tie peas in cloth with mint, allowing room for peas to swell.
2 Suspend bag in pan with boiling pork; boil for 1 hour.
3 Then take out, rub peas through sieve, mix in margarine and egg and seasoning.
4 Replace in clean cloth and boil with pork again for further 30 minutes.
5 Lift out pudding, unroll from cloth on to hot dish; serve pork and vegetables separately.

Belly of Pork can be boiled in the same way, but being thinner will not take so long. Allow 15 minutes to the lb. then test for readiness.

Salt Pork may also be boiled, but it should be soaked at least an hour before boiling; no salt should be added to the pudding. (Salt is not necessary when boiling pork, either salt or fresh.)

Pig's Fry

you will need:

1½ to 2 lb. pig's fry, consisting of portions of heart, liver, sweetbread and kidney	12 oz. to 1 lb. onions
frying fat	1 teaspoon powdered sage
	salt and pepper
	flour

1 Wash the fry and let it soak 1 hour in salted water.
2 Cut into equal sized pieces, after draining from water.
3 Place in well-greased Yorkshire pudding tin, add sage, salt and pepper and dredge with flour.

4 Cover with sliced onions; sprinkle with salt and pepper. Dot with a little fat or pork dripping.
5 Threequarters fill the tin with boiling water, cover with greased paper or foil and bake in moderate oven 2–2½ hours. Serve from the tin. The fry may be baked in ovenware glass dish if preferred.

Boiled Pig's Head

The pig's head should be salted by the butcher; for a small family half a head will be sufficient. Rinse head well; place in large pan with water to well cover, bring to the boil, skim well, then add a few peppercorns and mixed herbs. Simmer gently, 3½ hours for whole head, 2 hours for half. Meaty parts of the head and tongue are cut away from bone and arranged on a dish; brains are cooked wrapped in muslin when head is almost done. Serve with Mustard Sauce (see page 50) and Pease Pudding, if liked (see this page) boiled with the head.

Pig's Cheek

This is often cured and smoked when it is known as **Bath Chap**. Some butchers sell it ready cooked, but it can be cooked at home. The skin is well scored and the chap roasted as any other pork joint. It is more popular served cold, as being rather fat some people find it too rich to eat hot.

Savoury Baked Pork Chops

you will need:

4 spare rib or neck chops	2 medium sized cored and sliced apples
2 medium sized chopped onions	salt and pepper
2 medium sized sliced tomatoes	1 tablespoon tomato sauce or ketchup
2 large wiped and sliced mushrooms	2 teaspoons Worcestershire sauce

1 Wipe the chops and put in casserole; cover with onions, tomatoes, mushrooms and apples.
2 Season well with salt and pepper, add the sauces.
3 Cover and bake in moderate oven (355°F.— Gas Mark 4) for 40 minutes. Serve from the casserole.
Potatoes may be baked in skins in the oven at the same time.

Pork in Curry Sauce

you will need:

1½–2 lb. belly or neck of pork	¾ pint stock
1 oz. pork dripping or lard	½ teaspoon garlic salt (if liked)
1 large chopped onion	½ teaspoon ground black pepper
1 large sliced apple, cored but not peeled	1 tablespoon chopped chutney or seedless raisins
1 tablespoon curry powder	
1 tablespoon flour	

1 Wipe the pork; cut it into four portions. Melt fat in saucepan and fry lightly all over. Lift out.
2 Fry the onion in same pan until transparent; add apple and cook until soft.
3 Stir in the curry powder and flour and fry 3–4 minutes; add stock and stir until smooth and thickened.
4 Add remaining ingredients and replace the meat. Simmer 1¼ to 1½ hours with lid on pan. Dish up with sauce poured over the meat, accompanied by Boiled Rice (see this page) and sweet chutney, or Apple Sauce (see page 26).

Casseroled Knuckles of Pork with Boiled Rice

you will need:

4 knuckles of pork	salt and pepper
dripping to fry	½ teaspoon mixed herbs
1 large onion	¼ pint water or stock
1 large cooking apple	6 oz. rice
1 diced carrot	

1 Wash knuckles, dry them well, score the skins 3 or 4 times.
2 Put them in a saucepan with a little dripping, and fry lightly on all sides. Remove to casserole.
3 Chop onion, fry for minute or two in pan; peel and chop apple and add to onion, add diced carrot, stir well, cover pan and fry 3–4 minutes, shaking pan now and again.
4 Arrange this mixture around the knuckles of pork, season with salt and pepper and herbs.
5 Add water or stock, cover casserole and place in fairly hot oven. When boiling reduce heat to slow (350°F.—Gas Mark 4) and cook 1½ to 1¾ hours.
6 Twenty minutes before meat is done, remove lid from casserole so meat can brown lightly. Serve from the casserole with boiled rice.

To Boil Rice: Rinse the rice, then place in pan with salted water to well cover. Boil rapidly 8 to 10 minutes. Drain and rinse under running cold water. Allow to drain, then place in a buttered, shallow, fireproof dish and place low down in slow oven to dry out, stirring it from time to time.

Pork and Onion Dumpling

you will need:

8 oz. suet pastry (see page 62)	½ teaspoon powdered sage
	salt and pepper
3 onions	
1 lb. spare-rib or neck of pork	

1 Roll the pastry into a circle. Peel and slice onions thinly; cut pork into medium sized pieces, removing excess fat.
2 Put a circle of onion slices in centre of pastry; sprinkle with salt and pepper and half the sage.
3 Place pork on top, season with remaining sage and salt and pepper; cover with remaining onions.
4 Dampen edges of pastry. Gather edges up over the pork and onions and pinch them securely together on the top. Press gently with the hands to form a smooth, compact ball.
5 Put in centre of floured cloth, gather sides of cloth up over the top, and tie loosely, but securely with string. Boil for 2–2½ hours.

Root vegetables may be boiled in the same pan to make a complete meal.

Bacon in the piece

Bacon is the cured flesh of the pig. The sides of meat are cured in dry salt or in a salt solution – brine – for about three weeks when it can be sold as 'green' bacon. For smoked bacon the cured sides are simply hung above smouldering sawdust or wood chips for several days. Not only does this give the stronger flavour so popular in many parts of the country, but it helps to preserve the bacon. A ham is the hind leg of the pig, cut from the carcass before curing and then cured separately; gammon is the hind leg brine-cured while it is still on the bacon side. It is then cut off square at the top and is usually smoked. So strictly speaking it is wrong to call all smoked joints of bacon 'ham', though the practice has become general.

A joint of bacon is an excellent low-budget buy, delicious baked or boiled, eaten hot or cold, and a welcome change from the usual joints. Don't regard bacon as a meat to be cut in rashers for breakfast: try a joint of bacon for dinner with the usual vegetables.

The GAMMON is the choicest cut, therefore the most expensive. Being a big joint it is usually cut into smaller joints, the MIDDLE GAMMON being the best and most expensive. Even so, a gammon rasher about ½-inch thick, grilled or baked is good, solid, filling meat, and will serve three to four people. Only for special occasions would you buy a joint, weighing 4–5 lb. to boil or bake.

The other cuts of the gammon are **Middle Gammon, Gammon Slipper, Gammon Hock, Corner Gammon**; all these are equally good boiled or baked, eaten hot or cold.

Cheaper cuts of bacon are:-

Forehock – Again a large joint but can be divided into smaller cuts – Fore Slipper, Small Hock, Butt End.

Prime and Top Streaky – Can be boiled or cut in rashers.

Flank – Comes next to streaky; all these three cuts are good for frying with liver or kidneys.

Prime Collar and End Collar – Small, inexpensive joints, good for boiling or roasting.

Long Back, Top Back, Back and Ribs – Good, fairly lean joints, popular for rashers, but can be boiled or baked.

Short Back – What you get when you ask for back rashers for frying or grilling. It should be sliced thinly, setting 6 or 7. Not cheap.

Oyster – This comes next to long back: makes a delicious small baked joint, weighing usually 1½ to 1¾ lb.

To Boil Bacon or Ham

you will need, for 4 people:

2½ lb. forehock, collar, gammon slipper or long back	bay leaf 2 carrots raspings or golden breadcrumbs
1 onion stuck with 6 cloves	

1 If the bacon is smoked, soak it 2–3 hours. Take from water, put into pan with water to well cover.
2 Add the onion, stuck with cloves, bay leaf and carrots. Bring to the boil, skim and simmer 1 to 1½ hours until tender when tested with fork.

3 Take up on to dish: remove skin while hot. Sprinkle with raspings or golden crumbs. Serve hot or cold.

For a Crackling finish to Boiled Bacon:-
after removing the skin, sprinkle fatty surface with Demerara sugar while still hot. Place under red-hot grill or in top of oven until sugar melts and becomes crisp.

Boiled Bacon with Watercress Sauce

Boil bacon as described: take up, remove skin and place bacon on serving dish.

For the sauce: Make ¾ pint White Sauce as described for Caper Sauce (see page 23), using half milk and half water from boiling bacon. Finally chop 2–3 oz. cleaned watercress and stir well into the sauce. Season with a little pepper – no salt. Pour over the bacon on dish.

Boiled Bacon and Broad Beans

The beans should be fresh and young, before skins have had time to toughen. Shell 2 lb. beans: add them to the boiling bacon 15–20 minutes before the bacon is done. Take up bacon, skin it, place on dish. Strain the beans from liquor and serve them around the bacon.

Parsley Sauce is the usual accompaniment to this dish.

To make: Add 1 tablespoon chopped parsley to the white sauce as used for Watercress Sauce.

If fresh broad beans are not available, canned beans, which only need to be brought to the boil in the bacon liquor, make an excellent substitute.

Boiled Bacon with Butter Beans, or Haricot Beans

Soak the beans overnight, allowing 8 oz. to 4 people. Allow butter beans 30 to 40 minutes in the boiling bacon liquor, and haricots 25 to 30 minutes.

Baked Bacon or Ham

1 After the bacon has been boiled as described for Boiled Bacon or Ham for 45 minutes, take it up and remove fat.
2 Score the fat in lines diagonally across, about an inch apart: then score it in the reverse direction, making diamond shapes.
3 Insert a clove in the centre of each diamond. Stand bacon in roasting tin: sprinkle brown sugar all over fat: dribble a little golden syrup over the sugar.
4 Place in fairly hot oven (400°F.—Gas Mark 6) and bake 45 minutes, or until tender, and a good glaze is formed.

Other Glazes for Bacon or Ham

Ginger Glaze: Stud the half-cooked and skinned bacon with cloves. Mix 1 tablespoon ginger marmalade with 2 tablespoons ginger ale. Spread over the bacon: bake in hot oven until bacon is done and top crisp.
Cranberry Glaze: Melt 2 tablespoons cranberry jelly, add an equal quantity redcurrant juice or raspberry vinegar. Pour over skinned bacon in roasting tin: bake until done, basting with the glaze from time to time.
Pineapple or Apricot Glaze: Pour the juice from canned apricots or pineapple over the skinned, half-cooked bacon. Bake in hot oven until bacon is done, basting from time to time with juice. Take up on to serving dish; garnish top with sliced apricots or slivers of pineapple.
In all cases any liquor in roasting tin can be served as sauce.

Cider-baked Forehock: Cider Sauce

you will need:

3–3½ lb. forehock, boned and rolled	2 tablespoons soft brown sugar
one-third pint cider	cloves
	Cider Sauce

1 Soak bacon in warm water about 1 hour: rinse and put in pan with water to cover and boil gently 30 minutes.
2 Take up, remove rind, put bacon in baking dish.
3 Mix cider with half the sugar: pour over the bacon. Leave bacon to stand in the cider for about 20 minutes, basting it from time to time.
4 Give bacon final basting: sprinkle remaining sugar over top. Stick cloves evenly apart in lines across top.

5 Bake in fairly hot oven (400°F.—Gas Mark 6) for 30 to 40 minutes, basting from time to time, but for last 15 minutes do not baste.
6 Take up and serve hot with Cider Sauce.

For the Sauce:
Put cider, in which bacon was cooked, in a saucepan, making it up to ½ pint if necessary; bring to boil. Add a heaped teaspoon cornflour mixed to a smooth paste with a little cider. Stir until boiling again and sauce clears and thickens slightly. Cook 1 minute; pour into sauce-boat.
Apple Rings are often served with this dish (see page 26).

Back Rashers with Redcurrant Sauce

you will need:

4 long back rashers	2 tablespoons vinegar
1 oz. lard or pork dripping	1 teaspoon Demerara sugar
1½ tablespoons redcurrant jelly	level teaspoon dry mustard
	½ teaspoon paprika pepper

1 Remove rind and rust from bacon: fry the rashers in the lard or dripping. Remove them to hot serving dish.
2 Add the jelly, vinegar and sugar to the hot fat and stir until jelly and sugar are dissolved.
3 Blend mustard and pepper to a smooth paste with a little of the liquid in pan; gradually add this to liquid in pan.
4 Stir until boiling, then pour over the rashers. Half a redcurrant jelly square dissolved in ¼ pint water may be used if no redcurrant jelly is available.

Raisin Sauce for Grilled or Fried Bacon

you will need:

2 tablespoons soft brown sugar	4 oz. seedless raisins
level tablespoon cornflour	2 tablespoons vinegar
½ pint water	knob of butter

1 Blend sugar and cornflour with 2 tablespoons water; simmer raisins in rest of water 5 minutes.
2 Pour raisins and water on to blended cornflour and sugar.
3 Stir well; return to pan and simmer until clear and slightly thickened.
4 Add vinegar and butter, stir well. Coat cooked bacon with a little sauce; pour rest in sauce-boat.

Sweet-sour Beans and Bacon

you will need:

4 oz. haricot beans	½ tablespoon tomato sauce
½ pint water	
4 oz. streaky bacon	½ tablespoon chopped chutney or sweet pickle
½ tablespoon treacle or golden syrup	
	salt and pepper

1 Wash beans, soak overnight in ½ pint water; put into saucepan with water in which they were soaked. Add teaspoon salt.
2 Cook, with lid on pan for 1 hour, or until tender, adding a little more water if necessary.
3 Rind, trim, and dice bacon; put half in casserole and cover with half the beans; add rest of bacon and beans.
4 Pour in treacle or syrup, tomato sauce and chutney; sprinkle with a little pepper.
5 Pour in liquor from beans to just cover contents of casserole, adding more water or stock if necessary.
6 Cover casserole, cook in moderate oven (355°F.—Gas Mark 4) for 45 minutes to 1 hour, removing lid for last 15 minutes. Serve from casserole.

Little Bacon Dishes

you will need:

4 tablespoons chopped, cooked ham or bacon	about 3 tablespoons stale breadcrumbs
1 large tomato	3 oz. grated stale cheese
pepper and salt	4 eggs
½ teaspoon Worcestershire sauce	little butter or margarine

1 Butter 4 individual heat-proof dishes.
2 Put a tablespoon ham or bacon in each.
3 Quarter tomato, slice quarters and arrange on top of bacon or ham.
4 Season with pepper and a few drops of sauce.
5 Sprinkle a few breadcrumbs round edges of dishes making a border about ½-inch wide.
6 Break an egg into each circle of crumbs; season eggs with salt and pepper.
7 Mix grated cheese with rest of breadcrumbs and sprinkle on top of eggs.
8 Dot with small pieces of butter.
9 Bake in fairly hot oven until heated through and eggs are set.

Bacon Dumplings with Savoury Cabbage

you will need:
For the Dumplings:

4 oz. self-raising flour	1 teaspoon chopped
1 oz. bacon or pork dripping	parsley
½ teaspoon dried mixed herbs	3 oz. streaky bacon

1 Rub the bacon or pork fat into the flour (no salt needed).
2 Stir in the mixed herbs and parsley; dash of pepper if liked.
3 Rind, trim and finely dice the bacon; stir into flour, etc.
4 Form into firm dough with cold water; turn on to floured board and work until smooth.
5 Cut into 8 equal portions; roll into balls on board. Coat well with flour.

For the Savoury Cabbage:

1½ oz. dripping	1 teaspoon chopped parsley
rinds from bacon	
1 medium sized onion, finely chopped	pinch salt and pepper
	1 teaspoon brown sugar
1 lb. cabbage, shredded	¾ pint water

1 Melt dripping in saucepan, fry bacon rinds in it about 2 minutes, add onion and fry 4–5 minutes.
2 Remove bacon rinds, add water and bring to the boil.
3 Add shredded cabbage, parsley, salt, pepper, sugar. Boil with lid on pan 4–5 minutes.
4 Add the dumplings, cover closely and boil 20 to 25 minutes.
5 Put dumplings in vegetable dish and pour cabbage with all the liquid over them. Serve at once.

Baked Beans and Bacon

you will need:

8 oz. haricot beans	¼ teaspoon black pepper
8 oz. streaky bacon in the piece	4 tablespoons tomato ketchup
1 tablespoon dark treacle	1 tablespoon malt vinegar

1 Soak the beans overnight.
2 Cut rind and outer edges from bacon; cut bacon into roughly inch-square cubes.
3 Strain beans, put half in casserole, add bacon, then remaining beans, and water to come to top of beans.
4 Put on tight-fitting lid; bake in moderate oven 1 to 1½ hours.
5 Melt treacle in equal quantity hot water, add pepper, ketchup and vinegar; add to casserole.
6 Cook for further 1–1½ hours, stirring occasionally.
7 Serve from the casserole.

Bacon with Apples

you will need:

1 lb. collar rashers	½ tablespoon flour
2 medium sized chopped onions	¼ pint milk
3 large cooking apples	1 teaspoon chopped parsley
½ oz. margarine	pepper to taste

1 Remove rinds and edges from bacon; fry until crisp; take up.
2 Fry onions until transparent in bacon fat; take up.
3 Peel and core apples, cut into slices, fry lightly in bacon fat.
4 Heat the margarine, stir in flour smoothly, then slowly add milk stirring until smooth.
5 Stir over low heat until thickened; add pepper and parsley.
6 Put rashers on hot dish with apple rings and onions; pour sauce over; garnish with parsley.
7 Serve with haricot beans and potatoes baked in jackets (see page 46).

Bacon and Red Cabbage

you will need:

1 oz. dripping, pork if possible	dash of black pepper
8 oz. onions	¼ pint water
1 lb. red cabbage	6 oz. streaky or collar bacon rashers
8 oz. cooking apples	1 teaspoon chopped parsley
1 bay leaf	
1 teaspoon brown sugar	

1 Melt dripping in saucepan, peel and slice onions and fry until slightly golden.
2 Wash and trim outer leaves from cabbage, cut it in quarters, then into fine shreds, rejecting hard centre core.
3 Peel, core and slice apples. Add cabbage, apples, bay leaf, sugar and pepper to onion in pan.
4 Cover closely; cook for ½ hour, stirring occasionally; add a little more water if first lot boils away.
5 Rind and trim bacon; dip rashers in and out of boiling water to remove excess salt.
6 Place rashers and rinds on top of cabbage mixture and cook 15 minutes longer.
7 Remove rinds and bay leaf; pile cabbage mixture on hot dish and arrange bacon on top.
8 Sprinkle with chopped parsley and serve very hot.
If liked this dish can be cooked in a casserole in the oven, when it will take a little longer; in this case serve from the casserole.

Apple and Bacon Pudding

you will need:

8 oz. suet pastry (see page 62)	1 tablespoon chutney sauce
1 lb. streaky bacon	1 tablespoon tomato ketchup
4 oz. cabbage	pepper to taste
1 large onion	
8 oz. cooking apples	

1 Roll out two-thirds of pastry and line a 2½-pint size greased pudding basin with it.
2 Rind and chop bacon, finely shred cabbage, chop onion; mix all these together with the bacon; add pepper.
3 Peel, core, and dice apples.
4 Put bacon and vegetable mixture into basin; cover with the diced apples. Add the sauce and ketchup.
5 Roll out remaining pastry to form a lid; dampen edges of pastry in basin, put on lid of pastry, avoiding stretching it.
6 Cover with greased greaseproof paper, then with cloth or aluminium foil; steam for 2½ to 3 hours.
7 Serve from the basin.

Family Mixed Grill

you will need:

4 small lamb cutlets	4 tomatoes
4 chipolata sausages	4 oz. mushrooms
4 rashers collar bacon	salt and pepper
4 slices lamb or sheep's liver	a little melted dripping

1 Trim the cutlets of excess fat; prick sausages; remove rinds and outer edges from bacon.
2 Wash and dry the liver, and remove any skin or gristle.
3 Cut the tomatoes in halves crosswise; remove hard stalk ends; wipe mushrooms and remove stalks. Put stalks in grill pan.
4 Place all on the grid in grill pan; sprinkle with salt and pepper and brush over with a little melted fat.
5 Place under red hot grill until cutlets and liver are a good brown, then turn the cutlets, liver and sausages; it is not necessary to turn the bacon.
6 Brush the turned cutlets and liver with a little more fat and continue grilling for a further 3–4 minutes, until well browned.
7 Remove the bacon, tomatoes, mushrooms and sausages and keep hot.
8 Lower heat under grill and give the cutlets and liver 2 or 3 minutes longer to make sure they are cooked through.

9 Arrange all the meats on a hot dish; if liked a little water may be added to the sediment and fat in the grill pan, boiled up and served separately as gravy.

4 oz. of rump steak can be included, but of course this will make the grill more expensive.

Mushroom and Celery Pie

you will need:

4 oz. mushrooms	2 tablespoons stock or
large head celery	milk and water
4 oz. streaky bacon	little butter or margarine
about 1 teaspoon dried	6 oz. short pastry (see
mixed herbs	page 64)

1 Wipe the mushrooms – if fresh they need not be peeled.
2 Remove mushroom stalks; cut in smaller pieces if large.
3 Remove stalk end, leaves and rough outer stalks from celery, wash it well and cut into thin slices across.
4 Remove rind from bacon; cut into thin strips.
5 Fill pie-dish with alternate layers of bacon, mushrooms (including stalks), celery, sprinkling each layer with a pinch of mixed herbs.
6 Add the stock or milk and water, put a few dabs of butter or margarine on top.
7 Cover with a lid of pastry; mark the edges with a fork and decorate with pastry leaves. Brush over with milk.
8 Bake in fairly hot oven (400°F.—Gas Mark 6) for 10 minutes, then cover with greaseproof paper, reduce heat and bake a further 20 to 25 minutes.

Cooked minced beef or pork may be used instead of bacon.

Veal

Veal, on the whole, is an expensive meat, chiefly because it is usually in short supply. So far as flavour is concerned, it is the least flavoursome meat, requiring a lot of preparation and 'trimmings' to make it really palatable. At the same time, there are cuts of veal that are really quite cheap, and well within the reach of the housewife who has to plan on a small budget.

To make up for its insipid flavour, roast veal should be served with a rich forcemeat; as it is lacking in fat it is often combined with bacon or ham in cooking.

The flesh should be a very pale pink, and finely grained; if it is turning a brownish-red, it will not be tender or palatable, since the animal it came from was a little too old for a calf and not developed enough for a cow.

The prime joints of veal are:

Loin – For roasting or Veal chops.
Best End Neck – Excellent for cutlets, but may be roasted in the piece as for Best End Neck of Lamb.
Fillet Leg – Expensive, but a good, economical cut for a special occasion, as there is absolutely no waste. When roasted, it is best with the small bone removed and the cavity stuffed with rich forcemeat.
Escallops – Cut from the fillet they are particularly good. Cut them wafer thin, flatten with a knife, dip in egg and fine breadcrumbs and fry quickly in butter. Serve with forcemeat balls and sections of lemon to be squeezed over.

Inexpensive cuts are:

Knuckle – Very cheap, excellent for stews; often combined with knuckle end of ham or bacon to make cheap but excellent galantine, and veal and ham pies. Boil with root vegetables and a *bouquet garni*; when meat is tender remove it from the bones, but continue to boil the bones and the gristly sinews which are very gelatinous and produce a good jellied stock and can form the foundation of the best white soups, jellied consommé, and real aspic jelly. It should be strained and left to set in a jelly in the refrigerator.
Shoulder – Cheaper than the fillet; best end is suitable for roasting or braising; thin end is used for stews or pies.
Breast – Used for white stews and soups, or can be boned, stuffed, rolled and roasted, but requires slow cooking. Streaky bacon should be tied round the meat to keep it moist, and it should be well basted. Allow 20 minutes to the lb. and 20 minutes over in fairly hot oven.
Offal and **Other Parts** – The head, when well cooked can be a delicacy, especially the cheek portions.
Liver, the best obtainable, tender and sweet but so expensive it is a luxury.
Feet, not very meaty, but useful for savoury jelly making; calves' feet jelly is strengthening for infants and invalids.
Heart, can be stuffed and roasted as for Sheep's Heart (see page 24) or braised.
Kidney, more delicate in flavour and more tender than ox kidney.

Rich Veal Forcemeat

you will need:

½ pint measure fresh white breadcrumbs
2 rashers chopped streaky bacon, rinds removed
1 tablespoon finely chopped parsley
½ teaspoon mixed herbs
grated rind of ½ lemon
pinch of powdered mace or nutmeg
salt and pepper
1 small egg
little milk or stock (if necessary)

1 Mix all the dry ingredients.
2 Bind with beaten egg and a little milk or stock if necessary to make a stiff, crumbly mixture.
3 Use for stuffing boned joints: make Forcemeat Balls (see page 24) with surplus to be cooked in the roasting tin around the meat; with un-stuffed joints make all the stuffing into balls and place in roasting tin 30 minutes before meat is finished.

Roast Veal is served with thick Brown Gravy (see page 23).

Calf's Head Vinaigrette

you will need:

1 calf's head (be sure that tongue and brains are included)
1 sliced onion
large sliced carrot
½ chopped turnip
12 peppercorns
½ tablespoon salt
2 tablespoons vinegar
parsley and lemon for garnishing

1 Ask butcher to remove tongue, then split the head in halves: eyes and nozzle are discarded.
2 Remove brains, rinse well and put in basin of salted water. Rinse head in several lots of warm water, then leave in salted water at least 2 hours: soak the tongue with the head, after washing it.
3 Rinse head and tongue well; put into large saucepan with water to cover, add vegetables, peppercorns, salt and vinegar.
4 Bring to boil, skim and simmer 2 to 2½ hours, adding the tongue for the last 45 minutes.
5 Rinse the brains, put in pan of cold water, bring to boil, rinse under running cold water until cold, then remove dark membranes and any tubes.
6 Tie brains in muslin and suspend them in the pan with head and tongue for last 20 minutes boiling.
7 Take up head when done, remove meat from cheeks and neck end. Remove skin from tongue and slice tongue lengthwise. Cut brains in slices.
8 Arrange meat and tongue in alternate layers on hot dish: garnish with the sliced brains. Mask with Vinaigrette Sauce. Place in oven to get really hot before serving, sprinkled with chopped parsley and garnished with half-circles of lemon.

For the Vinaigrette Sauce:

4 tablespoons olive oil
2 tablespoons tarragon vinegar
1 teaspoon chopped capers
1 teaspoon chopped shallot or spring onion
pepper and salt

Put all ingredients in a bottle and shake well. If preferred, the sauce may be served separately in a sauce-boat.

Knuckle of Veal Casserole

you will need:

1 knuckle of veal 2–2½ lb.
4 rashers fat bacon
1 large onion
½ teaspoon dried sage
½ teaspoon salt
¼ teaspoon pepper
4 wiped and sliced mushrooms, medium size
1 tablespoon flour
½ pint stock or water

1 Have butcher chop knuckle into 4 pieces; wash it well.
2 Cut rinds from bacon, cut bacon into strips, fry them in saucepan until crisp.
3 Add chopped onion, sage, salt and pepper to bacon and cook until onions are transparent, stirring often.
4 Remove to the casserole; add the mushrooms.
5 Fry the pieces of veal in the bacon fat and juices in the saucepan, lightly on all sides. Remove to casserole.
6 Stir the flour into the juices in saucepan over low heat and when smooth add the stock or water, stir until boiling, then pour into casserole.
7 Cover and cook in moderate oven (335°F.—Gas Mark 3) for 2½ hours.

Forcemeat Balls, (see page 24), may be added to the casserole 40 minutes before veal is finished.

Minted Veal

you will need:

1 lb. pie veal, minced
4 shallots or small onions, peeled and chopped
2 oz. chopped mushrooms
½ tablespoon chopped mint
¼ pint stock or milk and water
2 teaspoons lemon juice
salt and white pepper to taste
1 beaten egg

1 Put all the ingredients except the egg into a saucepan: cook gently 15 to 20 minutes, stirring often.
2 Add salt and pepper: beat in the egg away from heat.
3 Butter a 1-lb. loaf tin: put the mixture in.

4 Bake in fairly hot oven (375°F.—Gas Mark 5) 45 minutes to 1 hour.

5 Turn out on to dish and garnish with fresh mint leaves. This is very good eaten cold; chill it well, then turn out on to meat dish; serve with a green salad. Lamb can be substituted for veal.

Chicken

From being an occasional buy for a special treat, chickens have become one of the most economical and useful foods for the family that has to be fed well on a small budget. At 3s. 6d. to 4s. 6d. a lb. for young, roasting birds, chickens are cheaper than prime meat, and with careful cooking and planning you can get 3 meals for 4 people from a 4 lb. chicken – roast, cold with a salad, and a stew or 'meaty' soup from the carcass and giblets. A boiling fowl, is a particularly economical buy; it is meaty, and the stock left from the boiling makes that most delicious of all soups: Cream of Chicken. Being fully-grown birds, boilers are always weightier than roasters and are fatter, but the fat should not be wasted; most of it should be removed and rendered down and used for frying where you would otherwise use butter, or even for cake making.

To Boil a Fowl

you will need:

1 boiling fowl, trussed by the poulterer	6 peppercorns blade of mace
1 lemon	2 or 3 carrots
1 onion	outer stalk celery or
3 cloves	½ teaspoon celery salt
2 teaspoons salt	Parsley Sauce (see
giblets	page 14)

1 If the bird is very fat remove as much as possible from inside and the giblets.

2 Rub the breast with cut lemon; put onion stuck with cloves inside the bird.

3 Wrap it in greased paper, then in aluminium foil. Place in deep saucepan, breast upwards. Put in the washed giblets, cover with hot water, add salt, simmer for 1 hour. Skim.

4 Add peppercorns, mace and vegetables. Simmer a further 1–1½ hours, according to size – 4 lb. bird will need 1 hour longer, 4½ to 5 lb. another 1½ hours.

5 Take up bird, wipe it dry, remove trussing strings and skewers. Serve with Parsley Sauce (see page 14) made with half chicken stock and half milk.

Boiler into Roaster To give a roasted flavour and appearance, after wiping the boiled bird dry, brush it over with melted chicken fat, or place solid chicken fat over the breast. Put in roasting tin, cover with well-greased paper, and place in hot oven for 25 to 30 minutes, removing paper for the last 10 minutes or so to get a good brown.

Forcemeat Balls (See page 24) may be cooked in the tin around bird. If liked, the breast of the bird may be covered with sliced streaky bacon, which can be served along with it.

It is important that the chicken is put into the oven immediately after boiling; if allowed to go cold it will be dry and tough.

Fried Chicken

This is one of the best ways of serving chicken, as it has all the flavour of roast chicken and there is no carving to do at the table. Only small, young birds should be cooked this way. If buying a whole bird, the poulterer will joint it for you into 6 or 8 pieces, but you can buy ready-jointed chicken and this is economical when you are serving only two or three people.

you will need:

1 young chicken, jointed (6–8 pieces)	1 beaten egg breadcrumbs (fine)
flour, seasoned with salt, black pepper and paprika (optional)	4–6 oz. cooking fat or oil or chicken fat

1 Toss each joint in the seasoned flour; chicken liver can be included.

2 After flouring, brush joints over with beaten egg, roll in fine breadcrumbs.

3 Heat the cooking fat or oil or chicken fat in thick frying pan; put in chicken pieces. Do not overcrowd pan.

4 Fry until undersides are brown, then turn. Cover and fry over low heat 15 minutes.

5 Uncover, turn chicken and fry 5 more minutes or until crisp. Chicken is done if, when pierced with a fork in thickest parts no pink juice runs out.

6 Drain pieces on kitchen paper, and serve on hot dish.

7 Pour off any fat left in frying pan, add a little stock to sediment, stir over low heat until boiling; pour through gravy strainer into sauce-boat.

Chicken Stew (From Old Bird)

you will need:

4 oz. chicken fat or pork dripping	6 green olives (if liked)
1 boiling fowl, jointed (6–8 pieces)	2 bay leaves
	$\frac{1}{4}$ teaspoon mixed herbs
flour, seasoned with salt and pepper	1 tablespoon flour
	teaspoon salt
2 large onions, sliced	$\frac{1}{4}$ teaspoon pepper
8 oz. tomatoes, quartered	4 oz. cleaned and sliced mushrooms

1 Heat chicken fat or dripping in thick deep saucepan; dredge joints with seasoned flour, brown on all sides in the fat.
2 Remove chicken from pan; add onions, tomatoes, olives to fat in pan, stir and fry 4–5 minutes.
3 Add bay leaves and herbs; sprinkle in the tablespoon flour, salt and pepper; mix well.
4 Replace the fowl; add sufficient water or stock to cover. Put lid on pan; simmer very slowly until joints are tender – 2–2$\frac{1}{2}$ hours.
5 When bird is nearly done, add the mushrooms; simmer 15 to 20 minutes.
6 Canned or frozen peas can be added a few minutes before end of cooking, and served with the stew.
7 Dish up the joints on to a large meat dish; arrange vegetables round it. Thicken the gravy with a little extra flour; coat the joints with it and serve rest separately.

Chicken and Mushroom Pie

you will need:

1 pint white sauce (see page 50)	salt and pepper to taste
	2 bay leaves
8 oz. cooked chicken, coarsely chopped	pinch mixed herbs
4 oz. mushrooms, cleaned and sliced	8 oz. short pastry (see page 64)
1 medium sized chopped onion	beaten egg to glaze

1 Let the sauce cool, then add the chicken and mushrooms, onions, herbs and seasonings. Mix well.
2 Roll out pastry to just under $\frac{1}{4}$-inch thickness. Cut out a lid to fit an oval 1$\frac{1}{2}$-pint pie dish.
3 From left-over pastry cut a 1-inch strip and press it on the dampened edge of pie dish.
4 Put filling in pie dish, moisten pastry edge with a little milk or water, put on lid, taking care not to stretch it. Press edges well to seal.
5 Knock up edges with back of knife blade, then with thumb press into flutes all round.
6 Brush over with beaten egg; prick pastry top with fork. Decorate with leaves or triangles cut from remaining pastry; brush these with egg.
7 Bake towards top of hot oven (445°F.—Gas Mark 8) for first 15 minutes, then at 380°F.—Gas Mark 5 for a further 15–20 minutes, until pastry is a good brown, and it is certain that filling has reached boiling point.

Chicken Mince

you will need:

1 oz. butter or rendered chicken fat	1 tablespoon cooked ham or bacon
1 oz. flour	good pinch mixed herbs
$\frac{1}{4}$ pint milk, salt and pepper	grating of lemon rind
$\frac{1}{2}$ pint measure minced cooked chicken	1 tablespoon browned breadcrumbs

1 Melt butter or fat, stir in the flour, slowly add milk; stir until smooth and boiling. Season with salt and pepper.
2 Add chicken and bacon or ham, herbs and lemon rind. Stir over low heat until boiling point is reached.
3 Pour into fireproof dish, sprinkle with browned crumbs. Bake in hot oven 8 to 10 minutes. Serve with toast.

Farmhouse Rabbit

you will need:

1 medium sized rabbit, jointed	salt and pepper
1 large onion	1 tablespoon chopped parsley
2–3 oz. pork dripping or bacon fat	1 teaspoon fresh thyme, or $\frac{1}{2}$ teaspoon dried
1 oz. flour	2 rashers streaky bacon
$\frac{1}{4}$ pint hot water or stock	3–4 oz. fresh breadcrumbs

1 Clean the rabbit well; soak in salted water about an hour.
2 Dry well; roll in flour. Shake off surplus.
3 Chop onion; heat fat in thick saucepan, fry onion lightly in it.
4 Stir in the flour and cook and stir for 2 minutes. Take pan off heat and add the $\frac{1}{4}$ pint hot water or stock.
5 Bring to the boil, stirring all the time. Season with salt and pepper. Pour into oblong baking tin or ovenware dish.
6 Add rabbit, parsley, thyme, bacon cut into strips, and salt and pepper.

7 Add hot water to just reach the rabbit joints, then cover with thick layer of breadcrumbs. Pour over a little melted fat.

8 Bake in moderate oven (355°F.—Gas Mark 4) 1¾ to 2 hours. Serve from the dish.

Maryland Rabbit

you will need:

1 young rabbit, jointed	little flour
4 oz. pork dripping or lard	1 beaten egg
salt and pepper	2–3 oz. fine white breadcrumbs

1 Soak the rabbit joints in salted water for about 1 hour; rinse and dry the joints.

2 Heat the fat in pan on top of stove; sprinkle rabbit joints with salt and pepper, dip in flour, then in egg diluted with 2 teaspoons water. Allow surplus egg to drip off, then toss the joints in breadcrumbs.

3 Place rabbit joints in hot fat and fry lightly on all sides; transfer to ovenware dish or casserole, adding fat from pan, cover with foil then with lid.

4 Bake 45 minutes to 1 hour in hot oven (400°F. —Gas Mark 6) according to age of rabbit, basting from time to time with fat. Add a little more fat if necessary. Serve with savoury white sauce (see page 50).

Cold Meats

When you are on a small budget for food you can't include ready-cooked meats very often, neither the sliced and sold by weight nor the canned or potted varieties. But though these meats are so expensive, they can be made at home very cheaply; in fact they can be a real saving in your housekeeping budget and at the same time bring variety to dinner, high tea or supper.

Sometimes, especially in hot weather it is a good idea to roast or boil a joint with the intention of serving it cold. In this case *don't* cut the joint while it is still hot. There is a great difference in the flavour of meat cooked and left uncut to go cold and the meat left over after serving it hot. When the hot joint is cut the juices flow from the cut side, so a lot of the flavour is lost and it won't eat so well cold.

When preparing cold **Boiled** or **Baked Ham** or **Bacon**, leave it to go cold in the pan or baking dish, after removing the rind.

Cold **Boiled Bacon** or **Ham** should be well drained when the stock is cold, wiped dry, and the fat side sprinkled with raspings or golden crumbs that can be bought in a packet.

Cold **Baked Ham** or **Bacon** (see page 30) needs no further attention after it has gone cold in the dish.

A **Boiled Fowl** (see page 35) is tastier and more economical for serving cold than a roast chicken. Allow to go cold in the pan; dry it well before putting on serving dish. Garnish with sliced tomatoes, pickled gherkins or sliced pickled walnuts, and parsley sprigs.

Jellied Lamb's or Sheep's Tongues

you will need:

4 tongues, salted or fresh	level teaspoon salt, if unsalted tongues used
1 diced carrot	water to well cover
1 sliced onion	1 teaspoon aspic jelly crystals, or powdered gelatine
small turnip, quartered	
chopped outside stick celery	
bouquet garni (see page 19)	

1 Prepare and boil the tongues as for Boiled Sheep's Tongues, (see page 25), with all the ingredients except aspic jelly or gelatine.

2 After skinning, arrange the tongues while still hot in a straight-sided mould, dish or cake tin, about 6 inches across, making two layers of the tongues; they should be a tight fit.

3 Dissolve the aspic jelly or gelatine in ¼ pint of the sheep's tongue stock; bring to the boil.

4 Cool the jellied stock, then pour it slowly into the mould allowing it to seep into all the spaces. Use about half the stock.

5 Leave for a time to allow the stock to sink well into the mould. Then fill up with remaining stock.

6 Cover with aluminium foil, then put in small plate or saucer resting on the tongues. Put weights in the saucer. Leave to go cold, in fridge if possible.

7 Run knife round between tongues and mould; invert mould over plate and shake to remove tongues. Serve with salad.

Pressed Pork

you will need:

3 lb. salt belly of pork	blade of mace
1 medium sized sliced onion	6 peppercorns
3 or 4 cloves	jellied stock

1 Soak pork for 2 hours in cold water. Rinse and place in pan with cold water to cover; add onion, cloves, mace, peppercorns.
2 Bring to the boil, skim and simmer 2½ to 3 hours or until fork goes in easily. Take up and drain well.
3 Remove bones while still hot; do not remove skin. Press pork into a neat shape, forcing it into a loaf tin or pie dish that just fits it.
4 Cover with aluminium foil and weight it down evenly on top of foil, using weights or heavy jars or tins.
5 Leave until cold, turn out on to serving dish, pour jellied stock over (see Jellied Lamb's Tongues); leave to set. Garnish with a little chopped jellied stock.

Pig's Head Brawn

you will need:

½ pig's head	*bouquet garni* (see page 19)
2 chopped onions	
½ tablespoon mixed pickling spice	1 teaspoon salt
	¼ teaspoon pepper

1 Have the butcher remove the snout and eye from the head, but retain the ear; see that the tongue and brain are left in.
2 Wash well, and soak the head in salted water for about 2 hours. Drain and rinse well in hot water.
3 Place in pan with cold water to cover, bring to the boil, strain, and rinse head under running cold water.
4 Replace in fresh cold water to cover, with onions, spice, *bouquet garni*; simmer 1½ to 2 hours.
5 Remove head from pan, cut all meat from bones; skin tongue and remove membranes from brains. Return bones to pan and boil rapidly for 1 hour to get a rich, reduced stock.
6 Cut meat, tongue and brains into small pieces, but do not mince, add salt and pepper, mix well; three-parts fill a mould or basin with it.
7 Cover completely with the reduced stock and leave until cold. The meat will rise slightly in the mould, leaving a good layer of jelly in the bottom. When cold and set run sharp knife round between brawn and basin, invert over plate and shake firmly to remove brawn.

Veal Mould

you will need:

1½ lb. breast or neck of veal	grated rind ½ lemon
6 oz. lean bacon or ham	level teaspoon salt
1 pint stock or water (if water is used add an onion and carrot)	¼ teaspoon black pepper
	½ oz. gelatine
	1 hard-boiled egg
bouquet garni (see page 19)	2 tablespoons cooked peas
2 teaspoons lemon juice	

1 Cut veal and bacon into roughly 1-inch square pieces, and simmer in the water or stock with lemon juice, *bouquet garni,* lemon rind, salt and pepper added, for 1 hour. Any bones from veal should be added.
2 Strain off ½ pint of stock and dissolve the gelatine in it. Allow to cool.
3 Pour a thin layer of jellied stock into a wide, shallow mould, let it half-set, then arrange sliced hard-boiled egg and peas. Cover with another layer of jelly; leave to set.
4 Fill up the mould with meat; slowly pour in jellied stock to just cover meat. Leave to set in cold place or fridge if possible. Turn out when cold.

Potted Beef

you will need:

2 lb. lean stewing beef or ox cheek	½ teaspoon anchovy essence
¼ teaspoon powdered allspice	¼ teaspoon black pepper
¼ teaspoon cloves	2–3 oz. butter or best margarine
¼ teaspoon mace	

1 Cut meat into small pieces, rejecting all fat; add spices.
2 Put in casserole with tight-fitting lid, add water to just cover, put on lid.
3 Bring to boil in hot oven or over low burner, then reduce oven heat to slow, and cook for 3–3½ hours.
4 Pound the meat well while still in the casserole, using the end of wooden rolling pin, a stone jar, or pestle, mixing in the anchovy essence and pepper while doing this.
5 Pot up into 3 or 4 small pots. Leave to go quite cold.
6 Melt the butter or margarine, remove any scum, and pour a film of butter over tops of pots; leave till butter sets. Serve with thin toast.

Lamb Loaf

you will need:

1½ to 2 lb. minced lean cooked lamb	½ tablespoon chopped mint
4 oz. minced lean bacon or ham (cooked)	4 tablespoons breadcrumbs
1 small minced onion	salt and pepper
4 skinned chopped tomatoes	1 beaten egg
	little stock or gravy

1 Mix lamb, bacon, onion, tomatoes and the mint; stir until well blended.
2 Add half the breadcrumbs, salt and pepper to taste, mix well then bind stiffly with the beaten egg and a little stock or gravy.
3 Well grease a 2-lb. oblong loaf tin, and coat it with the remaining breadcrumbs.
4 Pack in the meat mixture, pressing it well down. Cover with sheet of well-greased greaseproof paper or aluminium foil.
5 Bake in fairly hot oven (380°F.—Gas Mark 5) for 30 to 40 minutes, until thoroughly heated.
6 Leave to go cold, then turn out and serve with salad.

The loaf may be made with fresh, uncooked meat, but it will require 1¼ to 1½ hours cooking.

Pasta - Macaroni and Rice

Macaroni Hash

you will need:

8 oz. quick cooking macaroni	salt and pepper
12 oz. left-over cooked meat	½ tablespoon tomato sauce or purée
2 oz. dripping	grated cheese
1 medium sized onion	

1 Cook the macaroni 8–10 minutes in boiling, salted water; drain through colander.
2 Chop the meat fairly small, rejecting fat, skin or gristle.
3 Heat the dripping in saucepan; chop onion and fry lightly, about 5 minutes, stirring often. Put in meat.
4 Add the macaroni, with a tablespoon of the water in which it was boiled.
5 Season to taste with salt and pepper; add tomato sauce or purée.
6 Stir well until boiling; simmer 4–5 minutes.
7 Turn out into serving dish; sprinkle with grated cheese.

Note:
Any kind of cold cooked meat may be used; when preparing cold cooked meat dishes remember that the meat only needs *reheating*; over-cooking will make it tough.

Macaroni Casserole

you will need:

8 oz. macaroni	small tin baked beans in tomato sauce or 6 oz.
2 oz. dripping	haricot beans, with
12 oz. minced beef	tablespoon tomato
1 large onion, minced	sauce added
1 teaspoon salt	small can tomato soup
¼ teaspoon pepper	

1 Cook the macaroni in boiling salted water for 10 minutes; drain through colander.
2 If long macaroni is used, chop it roughly.
3 Heat dripping in frying pan; fry mince and onion lightly in it, adding salt and pepper.
4 Put a layer of macaroni in casserole, then a layer of mince.
5 Add a layer of baked beans or cooked haricot beans with tomato sauce added.
6 Add another layer of meat and a last layer of macaroni.
7 Heat the soup in the pan in which meat was fried; pour it over top of contents of casserole.
8 Bake in moderate oven (355°F.—Gas Mark 4), 25 to 30 minutes.
Spaghetti may be used instead of macaroni; it will need only 6–8 minutes boiling. Break it into short lengths.
If **short cut macaroni** is used it saves time as no cutting up is needed.

Savoury Pasta

you will need:

8 oz. macaroni or spaghetti
5 to 6 oz. minced left-over meat
8 oz. chopped onion
8 oz. finely chopped celery
8 oz. tomatoes
1 tablespoon grated cheese
1 tablespoon tomato sauce
¼ teaspoon pepper

1 Break the macaroni or spaghetti into short lengths; boil 10 minutes in salted water to cover. Drain.
2 Put minced meat in saucepan over low heat, add onion, celery and chopped skinned tomatoes, and 1 tablespoon macaroni water.
3 Simmer 15 minutes, stirring often; add the macaroni or spaghetti; mix well.
4 Add the grated cheese and tomato sauce, and the pepper, and more salt if necessary.
5 Make thoroughly hot; serve with extra grated cheese.

Note:

To skin tomatoes, dip them in boiling water for a second or so, then the skins can easily be removed with a knife.

Spaghetti with Tomato Sauce

you will need:

1 lb. long spaghetti
2 oz. butter or margarine

For the sauce:
2 tablespoons olive oil
1 small onion
1 clove of garlic (optional)
1 large can Italian tomatoes
1 tablespoon tomato sauce or purée
salt and pepper to taste
2 oz. grated cheese
extra cheese for sprinkling

1 Boil the spaghetti in a large pan of salted water for about 15 minutes. Drain through colander; pour boiling water over it to separate the strands.
2 Toss in the softened butter or margarine, lifting it well with two forks. Arrange it round the edge of dish to form a border; keep hot.

To make sauce:
1 Heat the oil in saucepan, add finely chopped onion and garlic clove (if used).
2 Stir and cook for 5 minutes until onion is golden; do not brown.
3 Add the tomatoes, purée and salt and pepper to taste. Stir well; bring to boil.
4 Add the grated cheese and mix thoroughly. Simmer for 10 minutes.
5 Pour the sauce in the centre of the spaghetti border. Serve with extra grated cheese for sprinkling.

Macaroni Italienne

you will need:

½ pint cheese sauce (see page 50)
6 oz. minced beef
8 oz. short cut macaroni
2 oz. can or tube Italian tomato purée
black pepper
3 oz. grated cheese

1 After making cheese sauce, add minced beef in same saucepan. Simmer 10 minutes, stirring often.
2 Cook the macaroni in fast boiling salted water 8 minutes.
3 Add the tomato purée and half the cheese to the sauce and minced beef; stir well; season with black pepper.
4 Drain the macaroni well; add it to the minced beef etc.
5 Cook over low heat for 5 minutes longer.
6 Turn into a hot dish; sprinkle with remaining cheese.
Extra grated cheese should be served separately.

Meat Cups with Noodles

you will need:

8 oz. noodles (flat macaroni)
2 pints water
teaspoon salt
2 oz. butter
¼ teaspoon pepper
1 medium sized can of peas (or frozen or fresh cooked peas)
8 thin slices luncheon meat

1 Boil the noodles with salt in the water until tender, 8–10 minutes. Strain through colander.
2 Return noodles to saucepan, add the butter, pepper and more salt if necessary; toss over low heat until all noodles are coated with butter. Put on a shallow dish and keep hot.
3 Strain the peas, if canned are used. Twist the slices of meat to form pointed cups, securing with tooth picks or cocktail sticks.
4 Arrange the meat cups on the bed of noodles and fill them with the peas.
If preferred the peas may be heated before putting into the meat cups.
Oblong pieces of boiled ham may be used instead of luncheon meat.

Spaghetti Bolognese

you will need:

1 medium onion	good sprinkling black
1 clove of garlic	pepper
2 tablespoons olive oil	12 oz. spaghetti
2 oz. chopped mushrooms	knob of butter
8 oz. raw minced beef	2 oz. grated cheese
8 oz. tomatoes, peeled	(Parmesan if possible)
2 tablespoons thick tomato	
sauce	

1 Chop onion and garlic finely; fry lightly in oil.
2 Add mushrooms, fry and stir 2–3 minutes.
3 Add meat, stir well, cook for 5 minutes, until well blended.
4 Chop tomatoes and add to meat, then add tomato sauce and pepper; mix well, cover and simmer 30 to 40 minutes.
5 While meat is cooking boil the spaghetti in salted water to well cover it, 10 to 15 minutes.
6 When tender, drain through colander, return to pan with knob of butter and sprinkling of black pepper, and toss with two forks over low heat.
7 Pile on to hot serving dish, pour the meat sauce on top and sprinkle grated cheese on top. Serve at once, with more grated cheese if liked.

Ham Macaroni Soufflé

you will need:

6 oz. short-cut macaroni	1 oz. butter
2 pints water	good pinch pepper
1 teaspoon salt	3 eggs
$\frac{1}{3}$ pint milk	6 oz. minced cooked ham
$\frac{1}{3}$ pint macaroni water	3–4 oz. grated cheese
heaped tablespoon	
cornflour	

1 Put the macaroni on to boil in the salted 2 pints water until tender. Strain, reserving the water.
2 Put milk and macaroni water on to boil; mix cornflour to a smooth paste with a little milk; when milk and water boils pour over cornflour paste. Stir until smooth.
3 Return mixture to pan, add butter or margarine and pepper. Bring to boil over low heat, stirring all the time until sauce thickens. Stand aside to cool.
4 Separate egg yolks from whites; beat egg yolks and add to cooled sauce; stir until well blended.
5 Add macaroni and minced ham to the sauce; mix thoroughly.
6 Whisk egg whites until a stiff, but not too dry, froth is formed. Fold this into ham and macaroni mixture.
7 Butter a deep pudding basin. Pour the mixture in; sprinkle with grated cheese. The dish should be only two-thirds full as it will rise.

8 Bake in medium oven (400°F.—Gas Mark 6) until well risen and golden brown—20 to 30 minutes. Serve at once.

Spaghetti Milanese

you will need:

8 oz. spaghetti	$\frac{1}{4}$ pint sieved Italian
2 oz. butter	canned tomatoes
2 oz. mushrooms	salt and pepper
2 oz. boiled ham	3 oz. grated cheese
2 oz. pressed ox tongue	(Parmesan if possible)

1 Put spaghetti in a large pan with 4 pints salted water, boil for 15 to 20 minutes, till tender. Drain, and rinse under cold water.
2 Heat butter in same saucepan, add cleaned and thinly sliced mushrooms, stir and cook 2 minutes. Add ham and tongue cut into strips.
3 Add spaghetti and sieved tomatoes to mixture in pan, season with salt and pepper, add 1 oz. of grated cheese and stir until well mixed. Reheat to boiling point.
4 Serve rest of cheese separately.

Vermicelli Savoury

you will need:

8 oz. vermicelli	3 tablespoons finely
3 tablespoons finely	shredded white cabbage
chopped onions	2–3 oz. dripping or
2 tablespoons finely	cooking fat
shredded carrot	salt and pepper
2 medium sized skinned	2 teaspoons chopped
and chopped tomatoes	parsley
4 tablespoons minced	grated cheese
cooked meat or bacon	

1 Cook vermicelli 3–4 minutes in salted water to well cover. Strain and rinse in cold water to separate strands.
2 Place onions, carrot, tomatoes and minced meat or bacon and 4 tablespoons water in large frying pan and cook 4–5 minutes.
3 Fry the shredded cabbage lightly in the dripping or fat in another pan, stirring until all the cabbage is coated; then cook for 2–3 minutes.
4 Add the strained vermicelli and fried cabbage to the other vegetables and meat, add seasoning and parsley and cook together until heated through.
Serve at once, with grated cheese if liked. (Vermicelli is a fine, thread-like pasta and needs only about 3 minutes cooking.)

Chicken Pilaff

you will need:

- 1 large onion
- 2 tablespoons olive oil
- 6 oz. uncooked long grain rice
- ¾ pint chicken stock (chicken stock cube may be used)
- 1 level teaspoon salt
- ¼ teaspoon ground black pepper
- ¼ teaspoon mixed herbs
- 2 oz. seedless raisins
- 1 tablespoon chopped, unpeeled cucumber
- 12 oz. to 1 lb. chopped cooked chicken
- 1 pimento, canned (as garnish, if available)

1 Chop onion finely and fry until transparent in the oil.
2 Wash and dry rice and add to the onion and oil; fry over gentle heat for 5 minutes, stirring all the time.
3 Add stock, seasoning and herbs, the raisins and chopped cucumber.
4 Cover and simmer gently until rice is tender (about 20 minutes) and liquid is absorbed, stirring from time to time.
5 Then stir in the chopped chicken, reheat, taste and adjust seasoning if necessary.
6 Turn out on to hot dish and garnish with strips of pimento—or sliced tomatoes may be used as garnish.

Italian Risotto

you will need:

- 12 oz. long grain rice
- 2 oz. butter or margarine
- 1 small onion, chopped
- 1 clove of garlic, finely chopped
- ½ teaspoon marjoram
- ½ teaspoon thyme
- 1 small can Italian tomato purée
- 2 large tomatoes, skinned
- 12 stuffed olives
- ½ lb. breakfast sausage (Italian, if possible)
- 4 oz. liver sausage

1 Wash, boil, and dry the rice.
2 Heat butter or margarine, fry onion and garlic in it, without browning—2 to 3 minutes.
3 Add the rice and herbs; stir over low heat until well mixed, then mix in the tomato purée.
4 Chop the tomatoes, and slice the olives; mix with the rice.
5 Spread the rice on a shallow dish and reheat in oven or over low burner.
6 Have the sausages sliced thinly. Form the slices into rolls and arrange them on top of the rice just before serving.

Stuffed Green Peppers

you will need:

- 4 medium sized green peppers
- 8 oz. minced cold meat
- 2 chopped onions
- 1½ tablespoons tomato purée
- 1 oz. butter or margarine
- 6 oz. rice

1 Cut tops from the peppers, about half an inch down; remove seeds and fleshy parts.
2 Chop up the fleshy parts of the peppers, mix with the meat, chopped onions and purée, and heat in a saucepan with the butter. Season with salt and pepper.
3 Cook rice in salted water to well cover and when soft, but not mushy, rinse under running cold water. Drain well.
4 Mix rice with meat mixture and fill the peppers with it, rounding off the tops smoothly.
5 Replace tops of peppers, stand them in a casserole with a little butter in the bottom.
6 Cover with casserole lid and bake in moderate oven (400°F.—Gas Mark 6) until peppers are soft.

Tomato Sauce or Purée (for keeping)

you will need:

- 6 lb. sound-ripe tomatoes
- 8 oz. sugar
- ¼ oz. salt
- pinch of cayenne pepper
- good pinch of paprika pepper
- 1 fl. oz. tarragon vinegar
- 1½ pints spiced vinegar (see page 81)

1 Wipe and slice tomatoes; cook in uncovered pan till tender. Rub through a hair sieve.
2 Return pulp to clean pan, heat, add sugar, salt, cayenne and paprika, stir till sugar is melted; boil gently, keeping stirred, till moderately thick.
3 Add tarragon vinegar and spiced vinegar, continue boiling gently and stirring frequently till sauce is of thick cream consistency; in judging consistency, allow for sauce thickening up while cooling.
4 While sauce is still hot, pour into hot bottles through a funnel, to reach 1 inch from top; cork down at once with new corks previously brought to the boil in cold water and boiled for 15 minutes. When sauce is cold, cut corks level with top of bottles, cover with wax, or put on screw tops.

Vegetables and Salads

The chief thing to look for when buying vegetables and salad greens is freshness. Limp or yellowing leaves on cabbages, Brussels sprouts, cauliflowers and lettuce denote staleness; tomatoes, which can be used as a vegetable or in salads should be firm-ripe. It is better to buy them a little under-ripe and keep them for a day or two before using. When buying cauliflower see that the flower sprigs are tightly formed, not bursting into feathery fronds. A fresh cauliflower should be sold with the green leaves on. These leaves are cooked with the cauliflower. Too often as the greens fade they are cut off, making it more difficult to tell whether the vegetable is fresh.

Peas and broad beans should have green, fleshy pods; they should not be wrinkled or, in the case of beans, turning black. With young broad beans, the pods can be eaten, the beans being chopped into one-inch pieces in the same way as French beans. When buying garden peas be sure that there is not a large proportion of immature, pealess pods among them.

French or dwarf beans should be fresh and crisp enough to be snapped into pieces with the fingers; runner beans are naturally larger than French beans, but you can usually tell when they are stale by their dull appearance and the obvious bulge of the beans inside the pods, and if when you snap one there is a skin inside, don't buy them; those skins never cook tender.

At the height of their season when the vegetables are at their best and cheapest, it is possible to have the main course mainly vegetable, or a substantial salad; cheese or eggs can be included to make the meal more filling and well balanced.

When vegetables are really cheap, or if you grow your own, try to have two or even three green vegetables with the main meal. The familiar 'roast and two veg.' is all too often potatoes and one vegetable – why not 'roast and potatoes and two veg.'? Or, alternatively, have a bowl of salad greens on the table to eat, with or without dressing, on a separate plate?

More use should be made of root vegetables; usually we think of them just as flavourings for soups, stews and casseroles but they can be delicious served as a separate vegetable. Dried vegetables (pulses) such as haricot beans, butter beans, peas, whole and split, when well cooked and served with a well-flavoured sauce are very good eating and economical.

Beetroot should not be considered simply as a salad ingredient, or just boiled, sliced and covered with vinegar as an accompaniment to cold meat; it makes a delicious hot vegetable, especially the small, baby beets, that are very tender and can be cooked and served whole. Large beets are best diced after cooking and skinning.

Chicory is another salady vegetable that can be served as a hot vegetable.

When buying spinach remember that it shrinks a lot in cooking; 2 lb. will be required to serve four.

Copy the Americans and now and again serve Vegetable Plates as the main course; with a thick soup and filling 'afters' they make a satisfying, appetising meal.

Summer Vegetable Plate

When the vegetable plate is to form the main dish of the meal, allow 3–4 oz. per head of each vegetable, such as:

garden peas	cauliflower or broccoli
French beans	sprigs
baby beets	small new potatoes
young carrots	broad beans

All the vegetables except beets and broad beans can be cooked in one pan, as they require the same length of time to cook. Broad beans and beets are cooked separately as they would discolour the other vegetables.

Garden Peas: After shelling rinse in cold water.
French Beans: Cut off stalk and flower ends. Small beans can be cooked whole; snap larger ones in 1–2-inch pieces.
Carrots: The smaller they are, the better. Remove tops and root ends; wash well.
Cauliflower or Broccoli: Break into small sprigs; wash well and allow to drain.
Put all these vegetables in boiling water to just cover them, adding salt. Boil gently 15–20 minutes.
Broad Beans: Shell and wash beans, put in boiling salted water to just cover and boil gently 15–20 minutes.

Baby Beets: Choose beets not more than golf-ball size. Remove leaves, but do not cut off the roots. Wash them, being careful not to break the skin. Put in boiling salted water to just cover them, cook gently for 15–20 minutes. Allow to cool in the water then remove skins; sprinkle with salt and pepper.

When peas, French beans, carrots and cauliflower or broccoli are tender, drain them through colander.

Arrange the vegetables in separate piles on a hot, round shallow dish, using the cauliflower sprigs as separators. Or the vegetables can be served on individual plates, using the cauliflower sprigs as separators.

Butter or a creamy sauce (see page 50) should be served with Vegetable Plates. Grated cheese, or nuts, chopped hard-boiled egg can be sprinkled over (or served separately) to give the protein necessary for a properly balanced main dish.

If large beets are used, clean and boil them as described, but allow 30 to 40 minutes according to size. Cut them into large dice *after* boiling and skinning.

All the vegetables are improved in flavour and food value if tossed in butter while still very hot.

Braised Celery

you will need:

2 large heads celery
salt and pepper
½ pint stock or vegetable water

2 slices streaky bacon
¼ pint thick brown sauce (see page 24)

1 Trim the celery, cut into quarters and wash well.
2 Put in a well greased, shallow fireproof dish, sprinkle with salt and pepper, and pour in half the stock.
3 Remove rinds from bacon, dice bacon and fry it lightly.
4 Put fried bacon on top of celery, cover closely and bake in hot oven (400°F.—Gas Mark 6) 30–40 minutes or until tender when tested with a fork.
5 Drain liquid from celery, add it to remaining stock and boil for 5 minutes to reduce it. Stir in the brown sauce.
6 Pour over the celery in dish; return to oven for 5–8 minutes to make thoroughly hot. Serve from the dish.

Braised Onions: Use large Spanish onions, allowing one to each person. Peel them, place in saucepan and bring to the boil; strain and rinse under cold water. Proceed as for Braised Celery, allowing at least 40 minutes.

Braised Chicory: Proceed as for Braised Celery, allowing 2 medium sized heads per person, and 25–30 minutes cooking time.

Scalloped Potatoes

you will need:

½ pint cheese sauce (see page 50)
1 medium sized finely chopped or grated onion

salt and pepper
1 lb. potatoes
1 oz. butter or pork dripping

1 Add the onion to the cheese sauce, seasoning with a little extra salt and pepper if necessary (cheese sauce will already be seasoned).
2 Peel and slice the potatoes thinly; sprinkle with salt and pepper.
3 Place a layer of potatoes in a greased fireproof dish, cover with sauce.
4 Repeat the layers, until all potatoes and sauce are used, finishing with a good layer of potatoes.
5 Dot with butter or pork dripping, cover, and bake in moderate oven (355°F.—Gas Mark 4) for 30 to 40 minutes, then remove cover, place dish high in the oven and bake for a further 40 to 45 minutes until potatoes are tender and lightly browned.

A grating of nutmeg on top of the potatoes before baking gives an unusual flavour.

A pinch of mixed herbs added to the Cheese Sauce is also a change of flavour.

Creamed Spinach

you will need:

2 lb. spinach
1 oz. butter or margarine
1 oz. flour
¼ pint milk

1 tablespoon top of milk
1 teaspoon salt
1 teaspoon sugar

1 Remove stalks and thick veins from spinach. Wash in several changes of cold water.
2 Lift spinach from water into large pan. No water necessary.
3 Cook steadily until tender, 10–15 minutes.
4 Drain and press well, then chop on a board.

5 Make sauce with butter, flour, milk and top of milk. (For method see page 50.) Add spinach purée.

6 Season with salt and sugar, mix well and make very hot over low heat. If necessary add a little more cream (top of milk) to make the consistency soft and creamy.

Stuffed Onions

you will need:

4 medium sized Spanish onions	2 tablespoons breadcrumbs
2 oz. minced cooked meat	little gravy or brown sauce
salt and pepper	raspings
pinch of mixed herbs	2 oz. dripping or cooking fat

1 Peel the onions, and boil steadily 10–15 minutes.

2 Remove from the water. Cut ½ inch from stalk end of onions, then with a spoon remove centres of onions.

3 Mix the meat, seasonings, and breadcrumbs and bind stiffly with gravy or sauce: add the centres taken from onions (chopped) to the stuffing.

4 Fill cavities in onions with the stuffing, smoothing tops into smooth curve. Sprinkle with raspings.

5 Heat fat in baking tin and put stuffed onions in it.

6 Baste them with a little hot dripping.

7 Bake in hot oven (400°F.—Gas Mark 6) 45 to 50 minutes or until quite soft when tested with fork.

8 Drain from fat, using perforated spoon. Serve very hot with Brown Sauce (see page 24).

Cheesy Stuffed Onion: Use grated cheese in place of minced meat.

Stuffed Tomatoes: Do not pre-cook. Remove stalk end and scoop out the pulp. Add the pulp to the stuffing as used for onions.

Onions and Tomatoes: May also be stuffed with Herb Stuffing or Forcemeat (page 34).

Onion Charlotte

you will need:

4 Spanish onions	2 oz. cooking fat, frying oil or margarine
½ pint milk	
¼ pint water	1 tablespoon grated cheese
1 tablespoon cornflour	
1 oz. butter	2 tablespoons fine breadcrumbs
salt and pepper	
pinch grated nutmeg and cinnamon	½ oz. melted butter
4 or 5 slices stale bread	

1 Cut onions into thickish slices, put in pan with cold water to cover, boil 2–3 minutes, then pour off the water.

2 Add milk and ¼ pint water to onions, and simmer 10–15 minutes or until onions are tender.

3 Mix cornflour to a smooth paste with a little extra milk, add to onions, stir until boiling and sauce thickens.

4 Add the 1 oz. butter, salt and pepper, nutmeg and cinnamon and mix well.

5 Cut crusts from bread; fry bread in fat, oil or margarine until golden brown, turning once: line a baking dish bottom and sides with it. Pour in onion mixture.

6 Mix grated cheese and breadcrumbs and spread on top; trickle the melted butter all over.

7 Bake in hot oven (400°F.—Gas Mark 6) until breadcrumbs are browned. Serve very hot.

English onions may be used, but Spanish have milder flavour.

If preferred, top may be covered with buttered bread, butter side upwards and grated cheese sprinkled over. Bake until cheese melts and browns.

Vegetable Pie

you will need:

1 medium sized onion, sliced	4 oz. haricot beans, soaked overnight
1 oz. pork dripping or bacon fat	2 tablespoons rice
	½ pint parsley sauce
2 medium sized carrots, diced	1 tablespoon tomato sauce or ketchup
1 small swede, cubed	6 oz. short pastry (see page 46)
1 medium sized turnip, cubed	

1 Fry the onion in the fat until transparent; boil carrots, swede and turnip and beans in salted water until tender. Strain.

2 Wash rice, tie in a piece of muslin, and boil 10 minutes in the pan with vegetables. Take out and rinse rice in running cold water.

3 Mix all vegetables and rice with the parsley sauce (page 50). Add tomato sauce or ketchup.

4 Place in pie-dish. Cover with short-crust pastry and bake in hot oven (400°F.—Gas Mark 6) for 20–25 minutes, until pastry is a good golden brown.

Serve with jacket potatoes.

For the short crust pastry:

6 oz. self-raising flour   ¼ teaspoon salt
3 oz. lard or cooking fat   cold water to mix

1 Rub fat into flour until crumbly, add salt, stir well.
2 Stir in with a knife, cold water to moisten, then with finger tips mix to a firm, elastic dough.
3 Roll out at once on floured board, to fit top of pie-dish.
4 Trimmings from pastry can be rolled out again and cut into triangular leaves to decorate top of pie.
Butter Beans may be used instead of haricot beans.
A small tin of **Baked Beans** in tomato sauce may be substituted for the haricot or butter beans and tomato sauce.

Jacket Potatoes: Scrub even sized smooth-skinned potatoes and remove all eyes or other blemishes. Dry potatoes. Prick the skins in several places. (This may not be necessary if skins have been cut to remove eyes etc.) Rub the skins all over with melted dripping, lard or cooking fat. Bake in hot oven 50 minutes to 1 hour, depending on size, turning them half-way through. Potatoes are done if soft when squeezed gently. As soon as they are done, remove from oven and make a cross-ways cut on top of each to allow steam to escape. If liked a knob of butter may be put into the cut. Serve very hot.

Vegetable Roll

you will need:

3 medium sized carrots   3 medium sized tomatoes
3 small parsnips   8 oz. suet crust
1 small swede   little Marmite
3 potatoes   pepper

1 Peel and grate carrots, parsnips, swede on suet grater; peel and thinly slice potatoes; skin and slice tomatoes.
2 Roll out suet crust into an oblong; neaten the edges.
3 Spread the vegetables evenly over the pastry leaving an inch uncovered all round.
4 Spread a small teaspoonful of Marmite over top of vegetables, and sprinkle with pepper.
5 Dampen edges of pastry; roll up lengthwise and press ends well together and the edge of pastry on top of roll.
6 Prick with fork in several places; put roll on greased paper on a baking sheet.

7 Bake in hot oven (400°F.—Gas Mark 6) for 1 hour, covering the roll with paper if it gets too brown.
Serve very hot.

For Suet Crust:

8 oz. self-raising flour   3 oz. shredded suet
¼ teaspoon salt   cold water to mix

1 Mix flour, salt and suet.
2 Mix to elastic dough with cold water.
3 Roll out on floured board to size required.

Haricot Bean Croquettes

you will need:

12 oz. cooked haricot beans   little milk
1 large grated onion   salt and pepper
½ tablespoon chopped   egg and fine breadcrumbs
   parsley   for coating
4 oz. breadcrumbs   fat for frying.

1 Mash the beans while still hot; mix with onion, parsley and breadcrumbs.
2 Make a stiff mixture with milk, adding salt and pepper.
3 Form into croquette (cork) shapes on a floured board; brush over with beaten egg, and coat with breadcrumbs.
4 Place croquettes in frying basket. Fry in lard or cooking oil until golden brown. (Fat should be deep enough to cover the croquettes.)
5 Take out of fat, allow fat to drip off, then drain croquettes on kitchen paper. Serve at once.
Butter Beans may be used instead of haricot beans.
Potato Croquettes are made in the same way, but be careful not to get the mixture too soft; use 1 lb. mashed potatoes.

Cauliflower-Cheese Puff

you will need:

1 medium sized cauliflower   1½ oz. fine white
2 oz. butter   breadcrumbs
1 oz. flour   3 eggs
½ pint milk   4 oz. grated stale cheese
salt and pepper

1 Wash cauliflower, remove stalk end, cut into quarters and remove inner stalk. Break into small pieces; boil in salted water until soft.
2 Melt butter in large pan, stir in flour until smooth paste is formed; remove from heat.
3 Warm milk and stir into butter and flour paste. When smooth return to low heat and stir until boiling. Season with salt and pepper, add 1 oz. breadcrumbs and simmer 3–4 minutes. Allow to cool slightly.
4 Separate egg yolks from white; add beaten yolks to sauce. Beat well. Add the grated cheese, and mix thoroughly.
5 Mash the cooked cauliflower and add to sauce, mixing well. Whip egg whites stiffly and add to mixture.
6 Pour into buttered casserole; it should be only threequarters full. Sprinkle remaining crumbs on top.
7 Bake in moderate oven (400°F.—Gas Mark 6) 30 to 40 minutes until well risen and brown. Serve at once.

Mixed Salad Bowl

you will need:

1 large, firm lettuce	salt and pepper
1 bunch watercress (2–3 oz.)	$\frac{1}{2}$ tablespoon olive oil
small bunch mustard and cress	1 hard-boiled egg
6 small spring onions	2 skinned and sliced tomatoes
1 sprig mint	2–3 inches cucumber
$\frac{1}{2}$ tablespoon chopped parsley	

1 Remove roots and faded leaves from lettuce, watercress and mustard and cress. Wash and wrap in towel to dry.
2 Remove roots and outer skins from onions; cut them into small pieces, using green parts as well as white. Chop mint with scissors.
3 Put onions, chopped mint and parsley into wooden salad bowl; sprinkle with salt and pepper.
4 Add outer leaves of lettuce, torn up, and watercress broken into small sprigs.
5 Pour the oil over and toss the salad with wooden spoons or salad servers until every leaf glistens with oil.
6 Spread these greens evenly in the bowl and arrange quartered lettuce heart round edge of bowl.
7 Decorate with slices of hard-boiled egg, tomatoes and sliced cucumber. Sprinkle with salt and pepper.

Serve French Dressing and Mayonnaise (see page 49) separately. To this foundation mixed salad other ingredients may be added to make main-meal salads.

For Vegetable Salad add grated raw carrot, white turnip, cooked diced carrots and peas, French and runner beans, broad beans – an assortment of these should be piled in the centre of the salad.

Vegetable Mayonnaise: Mix the vegetables with mayonnaise or salad cream; serve separately or pile in centre of mixed salad.

Fish Salad: 12 oz.–1 lb. cooked white fish, flaked, mixed with 2 or 3 chopped pickled gherkins, a teaspoon pickled capers and a tablespoon mayonnaise. Pile in centre of green salad.

Canned Salmon or Tuna Fish can be used in place of white fish.
Increase the number of hard-boiled eggs to have one for each person, for a main-dish **Egg Salad.**

Sardine Salad: Drain sardines from oil; split them downwards and remove backbones. Arrange the halved sardines with the tail-ends upwards and meeting around the pile of vegetables.

Apple, Nut and Celery Salad

you will need:

4 large red apples	2 tablespoons mayonnaise
2 oz. shelled walnuts	salt and pepper
2 sticks celery	$\frac{1}{2}$ firm lettuce

1 Rub the apples till they shine, remove 1 inch from the tops.
2 Core apples, and scoop out as much apple as possible leaving about $\frac{1}{4}$-inch thick apple case.
3 Chop apple removed from inside apples, chop nuts and celery, and stir them into the mayonnaise, adding a little salt and pepper.
4 Pile mixture into apple cases. Serve on lettuce either on large plate or individual plates.

Medley Salad

you will need:

1 large, firm lettuce	salt and pepper to taste
bunch watercress (2–3 oz.)	1 teaspoon chopped mint
4 large tomatoes	1 teaspoon chopped parsley
2–3 tablespoons diced	4 large sardines
mixed vegetables (cooked	few spring onions
carrot, peas, beans,	few extra cooked peas
summer turnip)	4 hard-boiled eggs
1 tablespoon mayonnaise	sliced beetroot and
dressing (see page 49)	cucumber to garnish

1 Wash and dry lettuce and watercress, removing coarse stems and faded leaves. Separate lettuce leaves; cut heart into quarters.
2 Cut ½-inch slice from stalk end of tomatoes, remove most of pulp and turn them upside down to drain. Chop pulp and add to mixed vegetables. Add mayonnaise and mix well. Season with salt and pepper and pile into the tomato cases; sprinkle with a little chopped parsley.
3 Split sardines and remove backbones.
4 Sprinkle chopped parsley, mint and chopped spring onions over bottom of bowl.
5 Add torn lettuce leaves and watercress sprigs, sprinkle with salt and pepper and salad oil. Toss until all leaves are coated with oil.
6 Pile peas in centre of lettuce and watercress and arrange sardine fillets round the pile. Put the four stuffed tomatoes at equal distances apart around the dish.
7 Cut hard-boiled eggs into quarters lengthwise and arrange around each tomato; put quartered lettuce heart alongside; garnish with sliced beetroot and cucumber.

Stuffed Apple Salads

you will need:

4 large dessert apples	6 chopped dates
1 tablespoon coarsely	1 heart of celery
chopped walnuts	mayonnaise dressing
1 medium sized banana	lettuce

1 Wash and dry apples; cut off ½-inch from stalk end, core apples and scoop out some of the centres, using curved grapefruit knife, or pointed knife.
2 Mix chopped apple centres with the nuts, sliced banana, dates and chopped celery heart. Moisten with mayonnaise.
3 Fill the apples with the mixture, piling it up. Put tops back on the mixture. Serve on shredded lettuce heart.

Crab-Meat Salad Cups

you will need:

4 small lettuces	2 hard-boiled eggs,
small tin crab-meat	sliced
mayonnaise	2 medium sized tomatoes,
4 tablespoons diced mixed	sliced
vegetables (canned)	1 piece chicory, quartered
2 tablespoons cold cooked	salt and pepper
peas	

1 With a sharp pointed knife remove the centres from the lettuce hearts leaving the larger leaves of the hearts to form the cups. Wash lettuce and drain well.
2 Drain the liquid from the crab-meat and mix it with an equal quantity of mayonnaise.
3 Chop crab-meat finely and mix it with the diced vegetables; moisten with the mayonnaise and crab-meat liquor; season to taste with salt and pepper.
4 Arrange the lettuce cups down the centre of a shallow oval or oblong dish; fill them with the crab-meat and vegetable mixture.
5 Decorate the dish with the lettuce hearts, the cooked peas, sliced eggs and tomatoes, with a quarter of the chicory at each corner. Sprinkle with salt and pepper, and serve with French dressing (see page 49).

Tuna Fish may be used instead of crab-meat.

Jellied Tomato Ring Salad

you will need:

1 lb. ripe tomatoes	1 teaspoon salt
medium sized sliced	6 black peppercorns
onion	1½ pints water
1 medium sized sliced	1 oz. powdered gelatine
carrot	1 tablespoon white malt
good sprig parsley	vinegar
2 bay leaves	lettuce and watercress

1 Chop tomatoes roughly, without skinning; put them on to boil with the onion and carrot, parsley, bay leaves, salt and peppercorns.
2 Boil until tomatoes are reduced to a mash, then strain through a sieve or Mouli grater.
3 Remove the carrot, parsley, peppercorns. Purée the tomatoes through the sieve into a saucepan.
4 Dissolve the gelatine in ¾-pint of the liquid in which tomatoes, etc., were boiled; make sure that all the gelatine is dissolved, then add the vinegar.
5 Mix with the tomato purée, heat to boiling point, then pour into a wetted ring mould.
6 Leave to set. Turn out on to a shallow round dish, garnish with a bunch of watercress in the centre of ring, and heart of lettuce leaves around the dish. Serve very cold.

Chicken Salad: Vinaigrette Dressing

you will need:

12 oz. to 1 lb. cold cooked chicken	few chives or spring onions
½ pint vinaigrette dressing	½ small cucumber, sliced
1 large or 2 small lettuces	4 small tomatoes, quartered
2 hard-boiled eggs	salt and pepper
	mayonnaise dressing

1 Cut the chicken into shreds, removing skin and bones; place in a bowl and just cover with vinaigrette dressing. Leave while preparing salad, stirring from time to time.
2 Separate lettuce leaves from hearts, wash and dry well; cut eggs into slices.
3 Line salad bowl with outer leaves of lettuce; shred lettuce hearts and toss in vinaigrette dressing. Arrange in centre of bowl. Sprinkle with chives or onions.
4 Drain excess dressing from chicken; pile chicken on lettuce. Arrange sliced eggs, sliced cucumber and quartered tomatoes around the chicken.
5 Sprinkle with salt and pepper; coat chicken with mayonnaise dressing.

for Vinaigrette Dressing

you will need:

1 teaspoon French mustard	½ teaspoon salt
1 teaspoon English mustard	sprinkling of pepper
1 teaspoon castor sugar	¼ pint white vinegar
1 teaspoon finely chopped shallot, or spring onions	¼ pint olive oil

1 Mix mustards, sugar, shallot, salt and pepper in basin. Add vinegar slowly, and mix well.
2 Add olive oil. Pour mixture into a bottle or jar with lid and shake violently for a minute or so; shake well just before using.

Fruit and Nut Salad

you will need:

¼ pint measure chopped pineapple, fresh or canned	2 tablespoons chopped nuts, any kind
¼ pint chopped orange, skinned and seeded	3 teaspoons castor sugar
4 oz. white grapes, skinned and seeded	little lemon juice
	mayonnaise
1 medium sized red apple, cored but not skinned, and and chopped	small lettuce
	1 small, finely sliced head of chicory

1 Mix the fruits; if canned pineapple is used, drain it well.
2 Add the nuts and sugar and mix well. Place all in glass salad bowl; sprinkle with lemon juice.
3 Add sufficient mayonnaise to coat the fruit without making it too moist.
4 Arrange well-washed and dried heart of lettuce leaves around bowl, and put the sliced chicory over the top resting on the mayonnaise.
Serve with French dressing (see this page).

Salad Dressings: Sauces
Standard French Dressing

you will need:

2 tablespoons olive oil	1 saltspoon salt
1 tablespoon vinegar	dash of pepper

Mix in a cup or basin and pour over the salad at time of serving.
This standard dressing – one-third vinegar to two-thirds oil – can be varied according to individual taste, and other ingredients, such as mustard, sugar, black pepper and paprika can be added; a little mayonnaise or sour cream, or plain yogurt is also liked by some people.

Egg Dressing: (Sometimes called English dressing). To ¼ pint French Dressing add ½ tablespoon finely chopped parsley and 1 hard-boiled egg, sieved or put through a Mouli grater.

Quick Mayonnaise

you will need:

½ pint white sauce (see page 50)	2 tablespoons olive oil
	½ tablespoon vinegar
1 teaspoon made mustard	
1 egg yolk	

1 Allow the white sauce to cool in the saucepan, then beat in the egg yolk.
2 Add the oil, blend well, then add the vinegar slowly, stirring all the time.
This sauce is improved if a tablespoon of cream or top of the milk is added, or evaporated milk can be used.

Tartare Sauce: Add 1 tablespoon chopped capers and 1 teaspoon chopped parsley to ½ pint mayonnaise.

Cooked Salad Dressing (for keeping)

you will need:

2 teaspoons flour
3 teaspoons castor sugar
pinch black pepper
1 teaspoon salt
½ teaspoon dry mustard
2 oz. melted butter
2 egg yolks
¼ pint evaporated milk
4 tablespoons white vinegar

1 Mix all dry ingredients, stir in melted butter, then the beaten egg yolks.
2 Stir until smooth, slowly add the milk. When mixture is smooth, put in top of double boiler, or in basin standing in pan of boiling water; stir over heat until sauce thickens.
3 Then gradually add the vinegar, stirring all the time. Cook until the mixture is the texture of thick cream that coats the back of spoon.
4 Pour into screw-top, sterilized bottle or jar; seal at once. Put a strip of Sellotape around bottom of screw-cap. Cool, and store in fridge. This sauce will keep several weeks if kept well sealed in the refrigerator, but *not* indefinitely. These quantities make just over ¼ pint.

White Sauce (basic recipe)

you will need:

2 oz. butter
2 oz. flour, sieved
½ pint milk
½ pint stock (vegetable or meat)
salt and pepper

Melt the butter, stir in flour gradually, away from the heat until a smooth paste is formed. Add warm milk and stock, beating well. Stir over low heat until boiling, simmer gently, stirring often, for 4–5 minutes.

Cheese Sauce: Add 2 oz. grated cheese to ½ pint white sauce.

For other variations to flavour sauce see page 14.

Sweet White Sauce: Mix 1 level dessertspoon cornflour to a smooth paste with a little of the ½ pint milk. Put rest of milk in pan with 2–3 inches of lemon rind, and 1 dessertspoon of sugar, and heat until milk is well flavoured with the lemon, about 8 minutes. Do not boil. Strain milk over the blended cornflour, return all to the pan and simmer 3–4 minutes. A little cream or knob of butter added at this point increases richness. Other flavourings may be added as you prefer.

Thousand Island Dressing

you will need:

¼ pint mayonnaise (see page 49)
½ tablespoon chopped sweet chutney
1 tablespoon tomato sauce
1 tablespoon chopped stuffed olives
1 small onion, finely chopped
2 teaspoons chopped parsley
1 chopped hard-boiled egg
3 teaspoons vinegar
4 small, crushed chillis

1 Put mayonnaise in a screw-top jar or bottle; mix the chutney and tomato sauce and add to the mayonnaise. Shake well in the bottle.
2 Add the chopped olives, onion, parsley, hard-boiled egg and shake well.
3 Mix the vinegar with the crushed chillis; add this to the contents of bottle and shake vigorously. Leave for an hour or so before using.
The dressing will get hotter the longer it stands; remove the chillis if you prefer a milder dressing, or use only two chillis.
The dressing will keep several days in the fridge.

Egg and Cheese Dishes

Eggs and cheese are the best friends of the woman who has to feed a hungry family on a small budget. With a good supply of them in the refrigerator or cool store-cupboard you always have the makings of good, savoury meals at hand; they keep well, so you needn't be afraid of keeping a good stock of them. Cheese will keep one to two weeks in the fridge so long as it is well wrapped, first in grease-paper and then in a polythene bag. Don't throw away any dried out bits of cheese: that is the best kind for grating.

Don't think of eggs as just something to use for a quick breakfast, or hard-boiled as a garnish in salad. Nor cheese as something to finish off a meal. Made-up dishes with eggs or cheese, or a combination of them can well take the place of meat as a main dish.

It is often taken for granted that anyone can boil an egg, but I have known quite good cooks who say: "I'll cook anything for you, but don't ask me to boil an egg." It is a case of the simplest thing needing the most care – and patience. Since soft and hard-boiled eggs are the beginnings of many savoury dishes it is worthwhile taking a little trouble over getting them right.

Hints on Soft-Boiled Eggs

Eggs for boiling should be new-laid, but not fresh from the nest; they should be at least 24 hours old, though eggs can be termed 'new-laid' up to a week, or longer if kept in a refrigerator.

Never put an egg straight from the fridge into boiling water; it is almost sure to crack. The eggs should be taken from the refrigerator at least 45 minutes before cooking. If this is not possible, put the eggs in a pan with *cold* water to cover them, bring to the boil fairly quickly then bring to rapid boil, put lid on pan, turn off heat and leave to stand 3 to 4 minutes, depending on individual taste. Or the cold eggs can be warmed slightly under running hot water and put into boiling water.

If the soft-boiled eggs are needed for making another dish, put them into cold water immediately they have been boiled the required length of time, to prevent further cooking.

As eggs go on cooking in the shell until it is cracked, they should be put in egg-cups at once and the tops cracked with a spoon.

Coddled Eggs: These are really soft-cooked eggs – that is cooked without actual boiling. Place the eggs in a warm basin, cover with hot water, stand the basin in a pan of boiling water, cover and leave for 8 to 10 minutes.

If a boiled egg is under-done – that is, if the white is still runny when top is removed, stand the egg in its cup in boiling water, with lid on pan for a minute or so.

Eggs Mollets: These are eggs that have been boiled one to two minutes longer than is usual for soft-boiled eggs and plunged into cold water when taken from the boiling water. The shells are then easily cracked and removed: the whites are firm but the yolks runny. The eggs mollets are then served on a bed of chopped vegetables such as creamed spinach, or garden peas, or minced cooked ham or beef. Sometimes tomato sauce or ketchup is served with them but is not really necessary, and to my mind spoils the delicate flavour of the egg yolk which forms a sauce in itself when the eggs are pierced with a fork.

Eggs Mollets in Aspic: Arrange the eggs mollets in a shallow dish; make a pint of aspic jelly by dissolving packet aspic jelly crystals in required quantity of water. When liquid jelly has cooled, but not set, pour it carefully over the eggs, coating them thinly and making $\frac{1}{2}$-inch deep layer in bottom of dish. Decorate the eggs with sprigs of parsley, thin strips of tomato and cucumber, mustard and cress, pressing them lightly into the soft jelly. Leave to set, then pour remaining jelly over the eggs, taking care not to disturb the decorations. Serve with salad.

Eggs Lyonnaise

you will need:

2 oz. butter or margarine	4 hard-boiled eggs, sliced
1 medium sized minced onion	1 tablespoon minced parsley
1 level tablespoon flour	salt and pepper
$\frac{1}{4}$ pint milk	buttered toast

1 Melt butter or margarine, fry onion until lightly browned.
2 Stir in flour smoothly, then add heated milk, slowly, stirring all the time. Bring to boiling point; simmer 3 minutes.
3 Add eggs, parsley and seasonings, heat thoroughly and pile on buttered toast.

Two tablespoons of chopped ham, tongue or chicken may be added to the sauce; be careful with seasoning when ham or tongue are used as they may be salty.

Eggs Benedictine

you will need:

4 soft-boiled eggs	2 tablespoons creamy
12 oz. cooked, flaked fresh	milk
haddock or cod	½ pint cheese sauce
½ to 1 oz. butter	(see page 50)
1 clove of garlic (if liked) or	little grated cheese
1 chopped shallot	triangles of fried bread
¼ pint white sauce	
(see page 50)	

1 Shell the eggs and leave them in warm water until wanted.
2 Melt butter in pan, add crushed garlic or chopped shallot, cook for a minute then add fish.
3 Add the white sauce slowly, stirring all the time, over low heat; when well mixed add the creamy milk.
4 Spread evenly on bottom of serving dish, drain eggs from water and arrange them on the fish.
5 Coat with the cheese sauce; sprinkle grated cheese over and brown lightly under grill. Arrange triangles of fried bread around edge of dish.

Hard-Boiled Eggs

Put the eggs in boiling water; boil gently 15 to 20 minutes. A hard-boiled egg always looks better when cut if the yolk is in the centre evenly surrounded by white. To get this, when the eggs have boiled for 3 or 4 minutes, turn them over and over in the pan with a fork, for a minute or so; leave them for another few minutes and repeat the turning process; repeat the turning at least once more, or as long as you have time and patience for.

When eggs are done, plunge them immediately in cold water; this makes it easier to remove the shells.

To remove the shells, roll the eggs between the hands to loosen shells, crack the shells and start to peel from the rounded ends of the eggs.

Eggs Mornay: Slice four hard-boiled eggs, lay them in fireproof dish, and pour ½ pint Cheese Sauce (see page 50) over the eggs. Sprinkle about 1 oz. grated cheese on top, dot with butter or margarine and brown under hot grill.

Creamed eggs or Fricasséed Eggs: Chop 4 hard-boiled eggs into eighths; put in pan with ¾ pint rich White Sauce (see page 50), reheat without actually boiling. Remove from heat, add 1 tablespoon chopped parsley. If liked a seasoning of made mustard or Worcestershire sauce may be added.

Mimosa Eggs: Cut 4 hard-boiled eggs in halves cross-wise, remove yolks, sieve them, and slice the whites. Put whites in hot buttered dish, pour ½ pint well-seasoned White Sauce or Cheese Sauce (see page 50) over them and sprinkle thickly with sieved yolks. Serve very hot.

Stuffed Eggs

you will need:

4 hard-boiled eggs	1 tablespoon tomato
salt and pepper	purée or sauce
about 1 tablespoon	1 tablespoon finely
mayonnaise sauce	chopped watercress or
(see page 49)	parsley
1 tablespoon grated cheese	a few fine white
	breadcrumbs

1 Shell eggs and cut in halves lengthwise; remove yolks and put in a basin.
2 Mash yolks with a fork, season with salt and pepper and mayonnaise; take care not to make too soft a mixture – whole tablespoon mayonnaise may not be needed.
3 Divide egg yolk mixture into three equal portions.
4 Blend one with grated cheese, one with tomato purée or sauce, and one with chopped watercress or parsley. Add a few white breadcrumbs if mixture seems too soft.
5 Pile flavoured yolks back into egg-white shells, using a spoon or fork. Sprinkle with a little chopped parsley.

Salmon or Sardine Stuffed Eggs: Add finely flaked canned salmon to the egg yolk mixture, taking care to remove all bones. Garnish stuffed eggs with diced cucumber.

Drain oil from tinned sardines, remove backbones and any fine bones; mash sardines with a fork, season with a few drops lemon or tarragon vinegar. Pile into egg-white cases; garnish with strips of tomato.

When using salmon or sardines it will not be necessary to use salt in seasoning.

Curried Eggs

you will need:

1 medium sized chopped	1 pint stock (bouillon cube
onion	may be used)
2 tablespoons olive oil	1 large cooking apple,
2 tablespoons flour	cored, peeled and diced
½ tablespoon curry	½ tablespoon
powder	Worcestershire sauce
½ teaspoon salt	4 hard-boiled eggs,
	sliced

1 Cook onion in oil until transparent.
2 Stir in flour, curry powder, and salt, and cook, stirring all the time until smooth stiff paste is formed.
3 Add stock slowly, still stirring, until mixture is smooth and boiling point is reached. Add apple.
4 Add Worcestershire sauce, cover, and simmer gently 15 to 20 minutes.
5 Add eggs, and let them heat thoroughly in the sauce. Pour into heated dish.
Serve with bottled chutney, and plain boiled rice.

Scrambled Eggs

you will need:

1—2 eggs per person   1½ oz. butter or
salt and pepper   margarine per egg
1 tablespoon milk to
  each egg

1 Beat eggs together until yolks and whites are well blended, season with salt and pepper and add milk.
2 Using a thick pan, heat the butter or margarine, pour in egg mixture and cook over moderate heat until egg begins to set around edges.
3 Stir with a fork, turning the cooked mixture into middle of pan so that uncooked mixture can take its place.
4 Continue stirring until all the mixture is set and flaky; remove pan at once from heat, stir thoroughly and serve on buttered toast.
It is important not to overcook the egg, or it will be tough.

Savoury Scrambled Egg: Fry a small chopped onion or shallot in the butter before adding the egg.

Minced Cooked Chicken, Ham, Tongue or Chicken Liver can be beaten into the egg mixture before cooking.

Grated Cheese can be added with the beaten egg; add a little chopped parsley when eggs are cooked.

A pinch of **Mixed Herbs** and a teaspoon of **Chopped Chives** or **Spring Onions** to each egg can be added while beating the eggs.

Shirred (Baked) Eggs

you will need:

1—2 eggs per person   salt and pepper
2 oz. butter or margarine

1 Break the eggs carefully into buttered individual ramekins or oven-proof dishes.
2 Put a little butter atop of each; season with salt and pepper.
3 Bake in moderate oven (355°F.—Gas Mark 4) for 15 to 18 minutes, or until set.
Shirred eggs are always served in the dishes in which they are baked.

Shirred Eggs Au Gratin: Mix equal parts grated cheese and fine breadcrumbs; add a pinch of dry mustard. Sprinkle on top of eggs in their dishes, just before putting in oven. Omit butter on top.

Crisply fried **Bacon Strips** can be put in the bottom of the dishes before putting in egg.

Swiss Shirred Eggs

you will need:

1 oz. butter or margarine   salt and pepper
3 oz. grated cheese (Swiss,   ½ tablespoon chopped
  if possible)   parsley
2 eggs

1 Spread the butter or margarine smoothly over a shallow fireproof dish big enough to take the eggs side by side.
2 Sprinkle over it half the grated cheese.
3 Break the eggs carefully on top; season with salt and pepper.
4 Mix rest of cheese with chopped parsley and sprinkle over the eggs.
5 Put in moderate oven (355°F.—Gas Mark 4) for 15 to 20 minutes, until eggs are set and lightly browned.

Note:
This is sufficient for one person for a main dish; the eggs may be baked in individual dishes if smaller servings (say for children) are required.

Cheddar or any firm English cheese may be used.

Fried Eggs

We usually connect fried eggs with bacon, and I think they taste best that way, but they can be fried in butter or pork dripping, on their own. But in whatever fat you fry them it is necessary to baste them to get a properly set, evenly fried egg.

Make sure the fat is hot, and deep enough to well cover the bottom of pan, so you can get a pool of fat at the side opposite the handle when you tip the pan. There is less risk of your getting splashed with hot fat, and of breaking the yolk if you break the eggs, singly, into a cup first. Slide gently into the frying pan towards the side opposite the pan handle, let frizzle until the white begins to set, then tilt the pan and with a palette knife or spoon baste the fat so it goes over the yolk, and there is no sign of unset white. Stop basting as soon as the yolk is covered with a film of set white. Take up with fish slice on to a hot plate; serve at once.

Turned Eggs: Some people like their eggs turned; in America they ask you how you like them – 'turned or flat'.

Fry the egg until it begins to set, and is lightly browned underneath, then with a fish slice lift the egg, make sure there is fat underneath, and turn the egg, and cook a minute longer. A well-turned egg is puffy and a good golden brown. Serve at once on a hot plate.

French Fried Eggs

These are deep-fried eggs – or eggs poached in oil in place of water.

A small thick pan should be used, big enough to comfortably hold one egg; a small saucepan or omelette pan may be used.

Put an inch depth of cooking oil in the pan. Place it over a low heat.

Break one egg into a saucer, season it with salt and pepper.

When the oil is hot (test by dropping a piece of potato in; it should rise to the top immediately) slip the egg carefully in. The white will begin to set almost immediately. With a perforated spoon pull the white over the yolk, entirely covering it. Then immediately turn the egg over in the oil, leave it for 2 or 3 seconds only, then lift it out on to a tea-cloth to drain. Transfer it to a hot dish and put where it will keep hot while the other eggs, if needed, are fried. French Fried Eggs can only be fried one at a time.

French Fried Eggs can be served with fried or grilled bacon, or as a separate dish, surrounding a dish of creamed potatoes, or Spinach (see page 44), or each can be set on toast or fried bread surrounded by tomato sauce.

They are also good with Macedoine (mixed diced vegetables) mixed with Mayonnaise Sauce, bottled or home-made (see page 49).

Poached Eggs

Poached in Saucepan: Have 3 inches salted water in shallow saucepan, or deep frying pan. Bring just to boiling point. Break one egg into saucer, slide gently into water. When white begins to set, lower heat, ease egg gently from bottom of pan with spoon; cook until white is set – about 3 minutes. Take up with draining spoon, drain off all water, serve on buttered toast.

Eggs may be poached in a special egg poacher, though this is really steaming as eggs do not come in contact with water.

The egg containers should be well buttered before dropping in the eggs. Have boiling water in the pan, put the containers in the holes in the top cover, put on lid and simmer until eggs are set, usually a little longer than when eggs are poached in water. Sprinkle a little salt and pepper on top of eggs. Release eggs gently from sides of containers and turn them out on to buttered toast.

Failing an egg poacher, use a frying pan with 3–4-inch pastry cutters in the boiling water. The eggs are broken into the cutters, and cooked until whites are set. Remove cutters when eggs are done, and take them up with a fish slice, allowing them to drain well before putting on to the buttered toast.

Bottled Tomato Sauce, or a Sweet Chutney Sauce can be poured over the eggs at the table.

Poached Eggs with Creamed Haddock

you will need:

2 golden haddock fillets
½ pint rich white sauce
(see page 50)

4 poached eggs
little chopped parsley

1 Place the golden fillets in boiling water while the sauce is being made. Do not continue boiling; fish will cook sufficiently in the hot water, with lid on pan.

2 When sauce is made, take up fish, drain it, then break up into small flakes, and stir into the sauce.
3 Pour sauce and fish into hot shallow dish; make 4 slight hollows around the top with back of tablespoon.
4 Place a poached egg in each hollow; sprinkle all over with chopped parsley. Serve very hot.
If liked, the sauce and eggs can be served in individual dishes.

Cheese Sauce (see page 50), may be used instead of the plain rich white sauce. In this case, sprinkle a little grated cheese, along with the parsley, on top.

Tomato Sauce (see page 40), may also be substituted, and a slice of tomato placed on top of each egg before sprinkling with chopped parsley.

8 Using a fish slice, or palette knife, fold the omelette in half, then holding the pan upright in the left hand, tip the omelette on to a hot plate. Serve at once.

For a filled omelette, put the filling over one half of the omelette before folding it. If preferred the filling can be put down the middle of the omelette and the two parallel sides folded over the filling. In this case it is easier to remove the omelette with a fish slice, as the omelette is liable to break while you are trying to work it towards the edge of the pan for tilting it out.

Note:
A frying pan should be kept for the sole use of making omelettes, and it should not be washed; a rub round with a piece of soft paper each time before using to remove dust is all that is needed. The pan will not be harmed if it is used for pancakes, but never fry meat, fish, etc., in the omelette pan.

Tip: A small nut of softened butter added to the beaten egg during beating will prevent any risk of sticking.

Omelettes

Plain Omelette

you will need:

For each person:

1 oz. butter, saltless if possible	1 tablespoon water as cold as possible
2 fresh eggs	salt and pepper

1 Put the butter to heat, in a thick 8–9-inch omelette pan, over low heat.
2 Beat the eggs with a wire whisk, long enough to blend yolks and whites.
3 Add the water, salt and pepper, beat again, lifting the mixture well up, to admit as much air as possible.
4 When butter is hot, but below smoking point, pour the egg mixture in, round the *sides* of pan (not plump in the middle).
5 Let the eggs cook until mixture begins to set round the edges.
6 Reduce heat, tilt the pan, and quickly draw the set portion of mixture towards the middle, allowing the soft portion to run to the edge of pan.
7 Repeat several times until all the mixture is set. Let the omelette 'rest' for a minute or two to brown evenly underneath. Turn off the heat.

Fillings for Omelettes:

Grated Cheese – sprinkle generously over half of omelette; after folding sprinkle top with grated cheese.

Spinach – freshly cooked, unchopped spinach, topped with a few dabs of butter added before folding the omelette; minced spinach with a little butter added during chopping can also be used; don't add dabs of butter.

Fish Omelette – add a good tablespoon of any cold white fish, finely chopped, and seasoned with a few chopped capers or chopped pickled gherkins, over half omelette after cooking. Sprinkle top with chopped parsley. Chopped, well boned sardines, mixed with a little tomato sauce can be used. Garnish with parsley sprigs.

Soufflé Omelette

you will need:

3 eggs
3 tablespoons water
salt and pepper

1 oz. butter, saltless if
   possible

1 Separate egg yolks and whites. Beat yolks; add water and seasoning.
2 Whisk egg whites stiffly; fold them into egg yolks with an over and over movement. Do not beat.
3 Melt butter in omelette pan; twist the pan so that the sides are greased. Spread the mixture lightly but evenly all over the pan.
4 Cook carefully over moderate heat without any mixing or stirring, until omelette is an even golden brown underneath.
5 Lightly brown top under grill; add the desired filling, fold and serve at once.
   Any filling used for plain omelette may be used.
   For **Sweet Soufflé Omelette** – omit salt and pepper; add half teaspoon castor sugar.
   For **Jam Omelette** – when omelette is cooked spread with warm jam, fold, put on hot dish; sprinkle with castor sugar.
   For **Apricot Omelette** – add grated rind of tangerine to egg mixture, omitting salt and pepper. When done spread omelette with sieved apricot jam or stewed apricots (sieved).
   For **Vanilla-Walnut Omelette** – omit salt and pepper; add a few drops vanilla essence to the water when adding it to the egg yolks. When done, sprinkle with a tablespoon chopped walnuts; fold and sprinkle top with chopped walnuts.

Main Dishes using Cheese

Cheese Soufflé

you will need:

3 large eggs
1 oz. butter
½ oz. sieved flour
¼ pint milk
salt and pepper

¼ teaspoon mustard
   powder
3 oz. grated Cheddar
   cheese

1 Prepare a 5-inch by 3-inch deep soufflé dish by brushing it well with melted butter. Grease a band of stiffish white paper long enough to go round the dish and wide enough to stand about 2 inches above side of dish; tie round the dish.
2 Separate egg yolks from whites. Melt butter in saucepan; stir in the flour.
3 Add milk gradually, stir until smooth paste is formed; continue to stir until boiling.
4 Cool slightly, then add egg yolks beating them well in; season with salt and pepper, and mustard.
5 Add grated cheese to mixture, stirring until it melts and blends with the sauce – avoid overcooking.
6 Whisk the egg whites until stiff and dry; fold into the egg sauce. Do not beat; there should be distinct layers of white showing.
7 Pour into soufflé dish; bake in moderate oven (375°F.—Gas Mark 5) 30 to 40 minutes, until well risen and brown. Remove paper and serve *at once*.

Cauliflower Cheese

you will need:

1 lb. cauliflower
¾ pint cheese sauce
   (see page 50)

1 oz. grated cheese
½ oz. raspings

1 Remove leaves from cauliflower (if fresh, these can be cooked separately for vegetable). Rinse cauliflower in cold water; level off stalk end.
2 Boil in salted water, flower side downwards, until tender. Take up with fork; drain on towel.
3 Stand it flower side upwards, in fireproof dish. Coat with the sauce; sprinkle with grated cheese mixed with raspings.
4 Brown in oven, or under grill. Serve with other vegetables in season.

Hard Boiled Eggs, cut in quarters, go well with this dish.

Tip: To avoid risk of cauliflower breaking during boiling, it is a good idea to push a long skewer through the stalk end and suspend the cauliflower in the boiling water, the ends of skewer resting on the edges of the saucepan; the pan lid will not fit tightly in this case but it is not essential so long as the water keeps boiling.

Cauliflower Sprigs may be used instead of the whole cauliflower. Break the cauliflower into sprigs or flowerets; wash them, drain, place in a strainer big enough to go into the saucepan; the cauliflower cooks quicker this way than when boiled whole. Lift out cauliflower in strainer when done, arrange flowerets in individual dishes and finish as for whole cauliflower.

Cheese Cutlets

you will need:

4 oz. fresh white breadcrumbs	1 egg
4 oz. grated Cheddar cheese	1 oz. raspings or golden breadcrumbs (packet)
salt and pepper	2 oz. pork dripping or 2 tablespoons cooking oil
½ teaspoon made mustard	4 short pieces macaroni
2 tablespoons bottled tomato sauce	parsley to garnish

1 Mix breadcrumbs and cheese, add salt and pepper and the made mustard.
2 Bind stiffly with the tomato sauce and half the beaten egg.
3 Form into cutlet shapes on a floured board, making four cutlets.
4 Add a teaspoon water to the remaining half beaten egg, brush cutlets all over with this, then coat them with the raspings or golden crumbs, patting them on firmly.
5 Heat dripping or oil in frying pan and fry the cutlets 4–5 minutes on both sides, or until golden brown.
6 Drain cutlets on kitchen paper; stick a piece of macaroni in pointed end of each to represent cutlet bone. Serve on hot dish; garnished with parsley.

Savoury Cheese Pie

you will need:

8 oz. short pastry (see page 64)	4 oz. sliced Cheddar cheese
4 oz. boiled ham	1 egg
2 medium sized tomatoes	¼ pint milk
salt and pepper	

1 Roll out pastry thinly, and line a 7-inch by 2-inch deep pie dish with it, using two-thirds of it. Press well down to bottom and sides, prick well and press again to exclude air.
2 Put a layer of ham in dish, cover with sliced tomatoes, sprinkle with salt and pepper, then cover with sliced cheese.
3 Beat the egg, add milk, season with salt and pepper and pour mixture over cheese.
4 Dampen edges of pastry lining dish, and cover with lid made from remaining pastry. Mark edges with fork and decorate top with pastry leaves made from trimmings.
5 Brush over with a little milk or beaten egg; bake in fairly hot oven (425°F.—Gas Mark 7) 25 to 30 minutes, or until pastry is well browned.

Cheese, Bacon and Egg Bake

you will need:

6 oz. streaky bacon	3 large eggs
½ pint white sauce (see page 50)	salt and pepper
½ tablespoon tomato purée	4 oz. grated cheese

1 Remove rinds and brown edges from bacon; fry rinds in frying pan to extract fat; cut bacon into strips.
2 Fry bacon strips until crisp; remove from pan.
3 Make the white sauce while bacon is frying; add tomato purée to it when it is made and mix well.
4 Add the bacon strips, simmer 2–3 minutes, then pour into shallow fireproof dish.
5 Beat the eggs, seasoning with salt and pepper, then add the grated cheese.
6 Pour over the bacon and sauce mixture in dish. Place in fairly hot oven (400°F.—Gas Mark 6) until egg and cheese mixture sets and browns lightly.
Strips of **Cold Meat, Tongue or Ham** may be substituted for the bacon, in which case they should be fried only lightly in a little dripping.
Canned Luncheon Meat is also very good.

Cheese and Bacon Tart

you will need:

6 oz. short pastry (see page 64)	pinch of cayenne pepper
4 rashers streaky bacon	½ teaspoon salt
3 oz. Cheddar cheese	4 tablespoons milk
2 eggs	

1 Line a 7-inch flan ring or tart tin with the pastry; prick bottom well, then press with fingers to expel all air and to close up the holes.
2 Remove rind and edges from bacon, fry bacon and cut into thin strips.
3 Spread these over bottom of pastry case and cover with thinly sliced Cheddar cheese.
4 Beat the eggs, add seasonings, stir in the milk.
5 Pour mixture into the pastry case, covering the cheese.
6 Bake in hot oven (425°F.—Gas Mark 7) for 10 minutes, then reduce heat to 400°F.—Gas Mark 6, and cook for a further 20 to 25 minutes until pastry is golden brown and the filling set.
If liked a little grated onion may be added to the filling.
Half a teaspoon Worcestershire sauce, and a grating of nutmeg instead of cayenne is another variation in flavour.

Cheese-Stuffed Baked Potatoes

you will need:

For each person:

1 large baked potato (see page 46)	½ to ¾ oz. grated cheese
½ oz. butter	salt and pepper

1 When potatoes are done, cut them in halves lengthwise.
2 Scoop out the potato, leaving the skins unbroken.
3 Mash the potato with a fork, adding most of the butter and grated cheese, salt and pepper.
4 Pile the potato back into the potato skins, forking it up neatly into a rounded pile.
5 Sprinkle remaining cheese over tops of stuffed potatoes, dot with remaining butter (use a little extra if necessary).
6 Place under red-hot grill until cheese melts and tops are brown.

Tip: It is really better to do the stuffing for each potato separately as this makes certain that the correct amount of potato and cheese is returned to each potato skin; it is quicker and easier to manage a small quantity at a time, and the potatoes can be kept hot during the preparation of each one.

Cheesy Snacks

Cheese Dreams

you will need:

1 level tablespoon mayonnaise or salad dressing	6 slices day-old ready-sliced bread (large size)
½ teaspoon made mustard	2 oz. butter or margarine,
3 slices processed cheese	or 3 tablespoons cooking oil

1 Mix mayonnaise or salad dressing with mustard.
2 Place a slice of cheese on 3 slices of bread; spread cheese with mayonnaise and mustard mixture.
3 Cover with remaining bread slices; press firmly together.
4 Remove crusts from sandwiches, cut in halves diagonally.
5 Heat butter, margarine or cooking oil in thick frying pan.
6 When fat is hot, put in sandwiches in one layer; fry until brown underneath; turn and brown second side. If sandwiches have to be fried in two lots it may be necessary to add more fat. Take up with fish slice; serve at once.

A sharp Cheddar cheese, or Swiss cheese may be used; in this case use 4 oz. and slice it very thinly.

Instead of mustard add ½ teaspoon Worcestershire sauce or a spicy, chutney-type sauce.

Cheese Popovers

you will need:

2 oz. flour	¼ teaspoon salt
1 egg	1½ oz. butter
¼ pint milk	2 oz. grated Cheddar cheese
½ tablespoon water	

1 Sieve the flour into mixing bowl, make a hollow in the centre and drop in the egg and stir well.
2 Add half the milk and beat until smooth paste is formed. Add rest of milk and the water and beat well, adding salt.
3 Put a knob of butter in each of a dozen deep patty tins; put in a very hot oven (450°F.— Gas Mark 8) for a few minutes to heat butter.
4 Put a teaspoon of grated cheese in bottom of each; two-thirds fill with the batter.
5 Return to hot oven for about 15 minutes, until well risen and golden brown. Serve hot.

Cheese Biscuits

you will need:

1 oz. butter or margarine	salt and pepper
1½ oz. soft grated cheese	pinch of dry mustard
2 oz. flour	

1 Cream fat and cheese, work in the flour and seasonings.
2 Knead lightly; roll out ¼-inch thick on floured board. Cut out into small rounds, ovals, squares, etc.
3 Bake in very moderate oven (335°F.—Gas Mark 3) for 15 to 20 minutes. Cool before removing from baking tray.

Anchovy Creams: Add ½ teaspoon anchovy essence when creaming the fat and cheese.

Anchovy Paste, or **Pâté** from a tube may be piped on to the biscuits, piling it up, or just making circles.

Other Toppings: Sliced hard-boiled egg, sliced stuffed olives on top of egg slice; grilled bacon; chopped boiled ham.

Cheese Straws: Roll out the pastry thinly; cut into strips $\frac{1}{4}$-inch wide and 3–4 inches long. Bake in hot oven until a pale brown.

Tip: It is easier to make the straws if you cut the pastry after rolling into a 4-inch wide strip. Put it on the baking sheet, and cut into $\frac{1}{4}$-inch strips, moving the strips slightly apart, so they will not stick together in baking.

Cheese Stuffed Tomato Roses

you will need:

3 large, firm tomatoes	salt and pepper
4 oz. cream or cottage cheese	lettuce or watercress
few stuffed olives (optional)	

1 With a sharp-pointed knife cut through the outer flesh of the tomatoes from the stem end downwards, in 6 or 8 sections according to size, leaving base uncut so that sections spread apart but remain attached.
2 Pull sections carefully open, remove a little of the pulp and hard centre core.
3 Add a little of the centre flesh, but no seeds, to the cheese; season with salt and pepper.
4 Fill centre of tomatoes with the cheese mixture; garnish with sliced stuffed olives. Stand them on a bed of lettuce or watercress.
Sliced pickled gherkins, or chopped cucumber may be used for garnishing instead of olives.

Stuffed Cucumber: Cut cucumber into $1\frac{1}{2}$-inch lengths; scoop out centres; chop centres and mix with seasoning, cream or cottage cheese. Pile mixture into cavities in cucumber.

Stuffed Dates: Remove stones from dessert dates and fill cavities with cream cheese, or wedges of Cheddar cheese.

Prunes: Stuff in the same way, after soaking and drying well.

Cheese and Ham Puffs

you will need:

1 oz. butter	1½ oz. chopped boiled ham or bacon
4 tablespoons water	
2 oz. sieved flour	1 teaspoon grated onion
2 small eggs	cooking fat or oil for frying
pinch salt and pepper	
3 oz. grated Cheddar cheese	

1 Put butter and water in thick pan and bring to the boil.
2 Put in flour all at once and beat until smooth and forms a ball.
3 Cool slightly then add one beaten egg and beat well until egg blends with ball of butter and flour, then beat in second egg, adding pepper and salt.
4 Add the cheese, ham and onion; mix thoroughly.
5 Heat fat or oil to low frying temperature (test by putting in cube of bread; it should brown in 1 minute). There should be 2–3 inches depth of fat.
6 Drop small teaspoons of mixture into the fat; fry to a golden brown, 3–4 minutes, turning them over with a fork now and again.
7 Take up with draining spoon, drain well. Sprinkle with a little finely grated cheese, and serve at once.

Cheese and Nut Balls

you will need:

8 oz. cream cheese	2 oz. chopped toasted almonds
2 oz. fine white breadcrumbs	salt and pepper

1 Press the cream cheese with a fork and add the breadcrumbs. Mix well, then add most of the chopped toasted almonds.
2 Season to taste with salt and pepper, then chill until firm.
3 Shape into balls with fingers dipped in flour, then roll the balls on a board sprinkled with the remaining chopped almonds.
4 Place on cocktail sticks and chill well before serving. Sufficient for 2–3 people.

Batters, Pancakes and Fritters

Yorkshire Pudding

you will need:

4 oz. plain flour
½ teaspoon salt
1 large egg
½ pint liquid – ⅔ milk
⅓ water

1 Sieve flour and salt together into basin.
2 Make well in centre and drop in the egg.
3 Stir to break the egg and add half the liquid.
4 Stir quickly, drawing in flour from sides until all is mixed in; beat until no lumps are left.
5 Gradually add rest of liquid, stirring at first until blended, then beat for a further 5–10 minutes.
6 Stand in a cool place for at least 1 hour.
7 Pour about 2 tablespoons dripping from roasting tin into a pudding tin about 10 by 10 inches.
8 Make it sizzling hot. Beat the batter again for 1–2 minutes then pour into the fat.
9 Bake in hot oven (425°F.—Gas Mark 7), towards top of oven, but allowing room for pudding to rise above tin, for 20 to 25 minutes.
10 Serve at once, cut in squares, from the tin.

Note:
A real Yorkshire Pudding should never be made from all milk; a little water makes it lighter; it should be made from plain flour, no baking powder added. It should stand at least 1 hour, to swell starch grains in flour, so pudding will rise quickly.
The batter can be baked in individual pans, but do not fill them more than half-full; this is a better way when the batter is served as a sweet pudding.

Yorkshire Pudding is traditionally served as an accompaniment to Roast Beef. In Yorkshire it is usually served separately, with clear beef gravy, as a first course, the meat and vegetables being then served on the same plate.
It can be served as a sweet course, with any kind of jam, honey, syrup, lemon curd or marmalade, poured over each serving.

Apple Batter: Peel, quarter and core 8 oz. apples; cut in thin slices and arrange in bottom of buttered pudding tin; there should be enough to well cover the bottom. Sprinkle with sugar; pour Yorkshire Pudding batter over. Bake in fairly hot oven (400°F.—Gas Mark 6) 35 to 40 minutes.
Stoned and quartered plums may be used in the same way.

Currant Batter: Add 3–4 oz. currants just before pouring the Yorkshire Pudding batter into the buttered tin, and bake in fairly hot oven 35 to 40 minutes.

Raisins or Mixed Dried Fruit may be added if preferred.

Savoury Yorkshire Pudding: Add a tablespoon grated onion, teaspoon chopped parsley, and a level teaspoon dried mixed herbs to the batter just before pouring it into the greased pudding tin. Bake in hot oven 25 to 30 minutes. This is often served in place of meat, with a thick brown gravy (see page 23), and vegetables.

Sausage Toad-in-the-Hole: Skin 12 oz. pork chipolatas; pour Yorkshire Pudding batter (same quantity as given on this page) into hot dripping in pudding tin. Arrange the sausages down the length of the tin. Bake 25 to 30 minutes in hot oven (425°F.—Gas Mark 7).

Note:
Skinless chipolatas can be bought, and save time and trouble.

Slices of Bacon, Pork, small **Lamb Cutlets, Kidneys** (skinned, split and cores removed), small **Slices of Liver,** can all be used for 'Toads', in the same way.
It is better to partly cook Pork slices, and Cutlets before putting them into the batter, as they may not be cooked through by the time the batter is cooked.

Pancakes

you will need:

½ pint Yorkshire Pudding batter
1 oz. lard or cooking fat
castor or granulated sugar
1 small lemon

1 Pour the batter, after standing, into a jug.
2 Melt the fat and pour into a cup.
3 Pour enough melted fat into a 6–7-inch frying pan to just mask the bottom; let it get smoking hot.
4 Pour a little batter into the pan, moving pan about quickly so batter spreads thinly all over the bottom.

5 Fry until a light brown on underside, then toss it or turn with fish slice and fry on second side until brown – 1 to 2 minutes.

6 Turn on to sugared paper, sprinkle with sugar, roll up and keep hot over pan of hot water until all are cooked.

7 Serve with cut lemon and more sugar.

Another way is to serve the pancakes unrolled and let each person squeeze lemon juice and sprinkle sugar generously over, and roll up.

Orange quarters may also be served for squeezing in place of lemon.

Or spread the unrolled pancakes lightly with **Butter** and sprinkle with Demerara sugar, and roll up.

Currant Pancakes: Sprinkle ½ teaspoon currants into each pancake as soon as it is poured into the pan.

Pancakes may also be spread with jam, honey, lemon curd, or marmalade.

Savoury Pancakes: Add to ½ pint Pancake Batter 2 oz. minced, cold cooked meat, boiled ham, or fried bacon and a dessertspoon minced or finely chopped onion, good dash pepper. Fry as for plain pancakes, but make them a little thicker, and fry for a minute or two longer.

Stuffed Pancakes: Spread pancakes, after frying, with previously cooked and warm veal forcemeat (see page 34). Roll up; keep hot until all pancakes are cooked.

Cheese and Apple Stuffed Pancakes: Grate 4 oz. stale cheese and mix with an equal quantity of grated apple; put inch-wide line of mixture down centre of fried pancakes, roll up. Put pancakes close together on dish so they will not unroll and place dish, covered, in moderate oven until stuffing is heated through – 5 to 8 minutes.

Cooked, Skinned Sausages can be rolled in the fried pancakes: or cooked **Sausage Meat** can be arranged in a sausage shape down centre of each pancake, and the pancakes rolled up.

Batter in a Basin: Grease basin thickly with butter; sprinkle bottom and half-way up sides with currants, pressing them well into butter. Pour in ½ pint Yorkshire Pudding batter. Cover with greased paper or aluminium foil twisted securely round edge of basin; steam for 1½ hours. Serve with castor sugar.

Jam or Marmalade may be substituted for currants.

Raisins or Mixed Dried Fruit can also be used.

Fritter Batter

you will need:

4 oz. flour	¼ pint tepid water
¼ teaspoon salt	1 egg white
1 tablespoon salad oil or melted lard	

1 Sieve flour and salt into basin; pour fat into centre.

2 Add half the water; mix until smooth, then add remaining water and beat 3 to 4 minutes.

3 Fold in the stiffly beaten egg white, and use at once.

Note:

This is sometimes known as French batter, and is used when an extra light coating for fish, meat croquettes or vegetables is needed.

It is also used for **Fruit Fritters:**

Fruits suitable:

Apples, peeled, cored and cut in rings.

Bananas, peeled and quartered.

Tinned apricots, peach halves, pineapple rings, well drained and dried in cloth.

Sections of oranges, pith, pips, and skin removed.

Oranges sliced across the sections, pips and shreds of skin removed.

Cook fritters in deep fat, lard or cooking oil; heated to just below boiling (or hazing) temperature. Immerse fruit in batter, lift out singly on a skewer, lower into the fat, making one layer. Fruit will rise to top of fat; allow to brown on underside then turn with fork and brown second side. When crisp and golden brown all over, lift out, drain well, and sprinkle with castor sugar. Serve very hot, at once.

Serve with Orange, Lemon, or Pineapple Sauce (see page 64).

Hot Puddings and Pies; Cold Desserts

In many families, especially where there are children, the 'afters' are often the most important part of dinner. For the housewife catering on a small budget this is a great help, since many hot suety or sponge puddings, or fruity or milky desserts, are fairly cheap to make, yet are very appetising and marvellous fillers-up for the ever-hungry ones.

Many of the fruity pies, tarts, flans and cold desserts are suitable for the sweet course, for high tea or supper.

When fruit is comparatively cheap (such as home-grown apples, rhubarb, gooseberries, plums), it is a good idea to make them into pies that can be served hot or cold; they go further this way, and make a welcome change from puddings that can be reserved for colder weather, when fruit prices soar.

Eggs, too, have their cheap season, and should be used as often as possible to make custardy, creamy sweets; their food value is high, and little skill is needed to use them for making something a little out of the ordinary for 'afters'. Don't be afraid of meringues, or meringue toppings, for instance; they are so easy to do and it is surprising how far two egg whites will go.

Basic Suet Crust for Steamed and Baked Puddings

you will need:

8 oz. self-raising flour, or plain flour with heaped teaspoon baking powder

$\frac{1}{4}$ teaspoon salt
4 oz. shredded suet
cold water to mix

1 Sieve flour, baking powder (if used) and salt; mix in suet.
2 Mix to a stiff dough with cold water. Use at once. For a richer, lighter crust, add an egg; adding it before the water. Less water will be needed.

Plain Suet Pudding: Turn crust on to a floured board; form it into a ball with fingers, working quickly and lightly. Put it into a greased basin, two-thirds filling it; press dough gently down to bottom and sides of basin. Put sheet of greased paper over top of basin, then tie on pudding cloth or twist aluminium foil well over rim of dish.

Stand basin in pan of boiling water to come two-thirds up the basin. Cover and simmer gently for 2 hours.

Turn out and serve with golden syrup, honey, jam, lemon curd or marmalade, on separate portions.

Tip: Suet pudding should be cut with fork and spoon to serve; never a knife. Don't take up the pudding until time to serve it. It should never be allowed to go off the boil. If first water boils away, replace it with more *boiling* water.

For **Spotted Dick:** add 4 oz. cleaned currants before adding liquid. Form into a roll, wrap in floured cloth, tie ends securely allowing room for pudding to swell. Place in pan of boiling water; simmer 2 to $2\frac{1}{2}$ hours, or steam in steamer over boiling water $2\frac{1}{2}$ to 3 hours. Serve with White Sauce (see page 50) or custard powder sauce, or with a pat of butter and a little brown sugar on each serving.

For **Boiled Jam Roll:** roll out crust on a floured board, fairly thickly, forming an oblong. Spread with jam to within one inch all round the crust. Dampen this uncovered crust, roll up, press edges well together. Wrap in floured cloth. Cook as for Spotted Dick.
Marmalade may be used instead of jam.
Mincemeat or a mixture of raisins and currants, sprinkled with sugar may also be used.

For **Baked Jam Roll:** proceed as for steamed Jam Roll, but do not wrap it. After rolling, place pudding in a shallow baking tin, brush top with milk, bake in hot oven (425°F.—Gas Mark 7), 45 minutes to one hour. Serve with Jam Sauce.

Steamed Fruit Puddings in Basin: Roll out crust about $\frac{1}{2}$ inch thick; cut out ring for top, using basin as guide; make remaining pastry into a roughly round piece, put it in greased basin, pressing it well to bottom and sides, right up to top of basin. Fill up with fruit, add sugar and a tablespoon of water, dampen top edge of crust and put on lid, pressing edges together. Cover with greased paper. Tie on cloth, leaving fold in top to allow for rising. Steam $2\frac{1}{2}$ to 3 hours. Serve from the basin, or turn out on to a plate.

Practically any fruit in season can be used in Steamed Fruit Puddings – **Apples** should be peeled, cut in quarters and sliced, removing core. **Gooseberries** topped and tailed. **Plums** are better with stones removed, though this is not necessary. **Black Cherries** are the most suitable type. **Dried Apricots** should first be soaked overnight. **Young Rhubarb** makes a delicious Steamed Fruit Pudding.

It is not necessary to serve a sauce with Fruit Pudding steamed in a basin, as fruit, combined with sugar makes its own juice.

Demerara sugar is the best kind to use; golden syrup may be used instead of sugar.

Basic Sponge Pudding

you will need:

4 oz. butter or margarine	pinch of salt
4 oz. castor sugar	1 tablespoon milk
2 eggs	
6 oz. self-raising flour, or plain with 1 teaspoon baking powder	

1 Cream the butter or margarine and sugar together.
2 Add eggs one at a time with a little flour, until thickened and smooth.
3 Add remaining flour, baking powder (if used) and salt, beating well. Add the milk, and beat again.
4 Well butter a 2½ to 3 inches deep pie dish or ovenware dish, pour in the mixture, smooth the top.
5 Bake in moderate oven (355°F.—Gas Mark 4) for 40 to 50 minutes, until well risen and golden brown. Serve cut in squares with jam or Jam Sauce (see page 64), or golden syrup, marmalade or Marmalade Sauce (see page 64). This mixture can be steamed in a well-buttered basin, covered with greased paper and aluminium foil twisted well over the rim of basin. Stand in a pan of boiling water to reach three-quarters up the side of basin, and steam for 1½ hours. Turn out of the basin on to a plate and serve as for Baked Sponge Pudding.

There are many variations to the Basic Sponge:
Sultana Sponge: Put 2 oz. sultanas in the bottom and round the sides of well-buttered basin, before pouring in the mixture.

Apricot Sponge: Add 3 soaked apricots, chopped small, to the basic mixture: put three or four apricot halves in the bottom of basin, stoned side uppermost, pour in the sponge mixture and bake or steam as described.

Jam Sponge: Put three or four teaspoons of any kind of jam in the basin; **Marmalade** may also be used.

Syrup Sponge: Put a tablespoon golden syrup in bottom of basin.

Castle Puddings: Put a teaspoon raspberry or strawberry jam in the bottom of dariole moulds (or any straight-sided individual moulds). Steam for 40 minutes or bake 25–30 minutes.

Chocolate Sponge: Substitute 1 tablespoon cocoa for 1 oz. flour, sieving it with the flour.

Ginger Sponge: Add 1 teaspoon ground ginger to the flour; use 4 oz. syrup instead of sugar, melted in warmed milk.

Black Cap Pudding: Put a tablespoon cleaned currants in the bottom of buttered basin.

Toffee-Apple Pudding

you will need:

2–3 oz. Demerara sugar	3–4 large cooking apples
1 oz. butter	1 tablespoon granulated sugar
6 oz. suet crust	

1 Press the Demerara sugar on to the sides and bottom of a well-buttered pudding basin.
2 Line basin with two-thirds of the pastry rolled out in the usual way.
3 Fill the lined basin with peeled, cored and sliced apple; sprinkle the granulated sugar among the apples.
4 Dampen edge of pastry in basin; cover with lid of remaining pastry, pressing edges well together; steam for 2½ hours.
5 Turn on to hot plate. The sugar pressed into the buttered basin will have melted to make a Toffee Sauce, but more Demerara sugar can be sprinkled on each serving if needed.

Apple and Mincemeat Pudding: Line the basin with suet crust, then put in a layer of sliced apple, sprinkle with brown sugar, then with fine breadcrumbs, then mincemeat. Fill the basin this way, cover with pastry, paper and cloth or aluminium foil, and steam 2–2½ hours.

Coconut Pudding

you will need:

4 oz. butter or margarine	8 oz. self-raising flour
4 oz. castor sugar	½ teaspoon almond
2 eggs	essence
4 oz. desiccated coconut	few blanched, split almonds

1 Cream butter or margarine and sugar until fluffy.
2 Add eggs one at a time, adding a little sieved flour between each egg; beat well after second egg is added.
3 Stir in the coconut, then add sifted flour gradually until a softly dropping mixture is formed. (Add a little milk if mixture seems stiff.)
4 Add the almond essence, mix well, and turn the mixture into a well-buttered basin, cover with greased paper and aluminium foil.
5 Steam 1¾ to 2 hours. Turn out on to serving plate. Cut the almonds into thin strips and stick these over the pudding.
Serve with **White Sauce** (see page 50), flavoured with a few drops of almond essence.

Sauces for Steamed and Baked Puddings

Jam Sauce:

1 tablespoon any jam, preferably red	1 teaspoon sugar
½ pint water or fruit juice	level teaspoon cornflour

1 Place jam, water or juice in saucepan, bring to boil.
2 Add sugar, strain and return to pan.
3 Add cornflour mixed to smooth paste with a little water, simmer 3 minutes until sauce thickens and clears.

Marmalade Sauce: Substitute chopped marmalade for jam.

Pineapple Sauce: Use juice from canned pineapple instead of water and omit sugar; add a teaspoon finely chopped pineapple.

Orange Sauce:

1 large orange	½ tablespoon cornflour
1 tablespoon sugar	½ pint water
1 oz. butter	1 egg yolk

1 Grate orange rind and mix with sugar.
2 Melt butter in saucepan, stir in cornflour, then add water slowly, and stir until boiling.
3 Add orange rind and sugar, and juice of the orange.
4 Simmer 2–3 minutes; cool a little then stir in beaten egg yolk.

Lemon Sauce: Substitute one large lemon for orange and add a little more sugar.

Hot Chocolate Sauce:

2 oz. plain chocolate	2 teaspoons cornflour
1 oz. castor sugar	½ teaspoon vanilla essence
½ pint water	

1 Melt the chocolate and sugar in the water; blend cornflour and add to mixture.
2 Stir until boiling, then simmer 2 minutes. Add essence and use. A small knob of butter may be added for a richer sauce.

Pastry Desserts

Points about Pastry

Flour must be absolutely dry, and sieved. Plain flour is best, though self-raising may be used for short pastry, when less shortening is used.
All utensils must be quite cold.
Work lightly and quickly; when rubbing in fat (shortening) lift ingredients, so flour, etc., trickles through the fingers to let air in.
Always bake pastry in a hot oven.

Short Pastry

you will need:

8 oz. plain flour	OR:
4 oz. shortening (lard, or mixture lard and margarine, pork dripping, or half butter and margarine)	4 oz. plain flour
	4 oz. self-raising flour
	3 oz. shortening
½ teaspoon salt	
OR:	
3 oz. shortening, plus ½ teaspoon baking powder to plain flour, or	
8 oz. self-raising flour	

1 Rub shortening into dry ingredients, until mixture is crumbly.
2 Mix to stiff dough with cold water.
3 Knead lightly until smooth.
4 Roll out at once and use as required.
5 Bake in fairly hot oven (400°F.—Gas Mark 6) until pastry is set; then reduce heat to finish.

Biscuit Crust

you will need:

6 oz. plain flour	pinch salt
3 oz. butter or margarine	1 egg yolk
2 teaspoons castor sugar	cold water to mix

1 Rub butter or margarine into sieved flour.
2 Add sugar and pinch salt.
3 Beat egg yolk with a little water; add to dry mixture.
4 Mix to a pliable dough with cold water; roll out and use at once, for sweet pies, tarts or flans.

Baking Blind

When a fresh fruit filling, canned fruit, jelly or cream filling is to be used, the pastry case must be made first, without filling. This is known as 'Baking Blind'.

Roll out short or biscuit crust thinly; the quantities given above are sufficient for two 8 by 1¼-inch deep pie tins. Halve the quantities for one pastry case.

Line the tin without stretching the pastry; press it firmly down to bottom and sides, pressing it into the angle between bottom and sides with back of fore-finger so it fits snugly. Prick bottom and sides with fork, and press again to expel all air.

Put a sheet of grease-proof paper in the bottom, cover this with dried peas or beans, or breadcrusts. Bake in hot oven (450°F.—Gas Mark 8) until golden brown. Remove paper, etc., return case to oven for a few minutes to allow pastry in bottom to dry.

Let the case go cold before using; Pastry cases can be made in advance and kept in an airtight tin.

Chocolate Cream Pie

you will need:

8-inch pastry case	2 eggs, yolks and
1 level tablespoon	whites separated
chocolate cornflour or	2 oz. chocolate dots, or
blancmange powder	drops
½ pint milk	chocolate dots for
1½ tablespoons castor	decoration
sugar	

1 Put the pastry case on serving plate.
2 Blend cornflour with a little milk from the ½ pint.
3 Put remaining milk on to boil in saucepan; when boiling pour over blended cornflour, stirring until smooth.
4 Return all to pan and stir until boiling; leave to cool slightly, then add a tablespoon of the sugar, and beaten egg yolks; whip well over low heat until thickened.
5 Remove from heat and mix in the chocolate dots or drops.
6 When the mixture has cooled a little, pour it into the pastry case and leave to go quite cold.
7 Then whip egg whites until stiff, adding remaining sugar slowly.
8 When chocolate filling is quite cold put the whipped egg white in small heaps on top, and put a chocolate dot on top of each heap. Serve as soon as possible.

Tip: It is best to leave the whipping of the egg white and placing it on top of the pie, until the last minute, as the egg white, not being cooked, may lose its puffiness if kept waiting.

Peach Special

you will need:

8-inch pastry case made	1 heaped teaspoon
with biscuit crust	cornflour
1 large can sliced peaches	

1 Put the pastry case on serving plate; drain the peaches.
2 While the peaches are draining, heat the syrup – there should be ¼ pint.
3 Blend the cornflour with a little peach syrup; when syrup in pan reaches boiling point, pour in blended cornflour, and stir over low heat until syrup clears and thickens slightly.
4 Arrange the peach slices in circles in the pastry case, allowing each slice to overlap the previous one.
5 When the syrup has cooled, pour it over the peaches to just mask them; serve at once before syrup has time to soak into the pastry.

This is an excellent last minute dessert for a special occasion, if you have the pastry case in store, and your special occasion shelf is well stocked.

A few chopped blanched almonds can be sprinkled over the top.

Canned Apricot Halves may be substituted, arranging them in one layer, rounded sides uppermost.

Strawberry and Apple Tart

you will need:

6 oz. short or biscuit crust (made with 6 oz. flour, 3 oz. butter or margarine)	1 heaped tablespoon sugar little water
12 oz. cooking apples	½ oz. butter
	6–8 oz. strawberries

1 Roll out the pastry to about ¼-inch thickness, to fit 8-inch tart tin.
2 Line tart tin with pastry; trim it and reserve cut off pastry to make lattice strips.
3 Peel, core and slice apples, stew them with the sugar and very little water until quite soft.
4 Beat apples to a purée, adding the butter. Put into pastry-lined tart tin.
5 Roll out remaining pastry and with a pastry wheel or sharp knife cut into strips ¼-inch wide.
6 Arrange strips on top of pastry, making 1-inch squares, dampening ends to make them stick.
7 Bake in hot oven (425°F.—Gas Mark 7) for 15 to 20 minutes until pastry is a golden brown.
8 Remove stalks from strawberries; wipe the berries.
   When the pie is quite cold put a perfect berry in each square.

Stoned Cherries can be substituted to make Cherry and Apple Tart.

Apple Amber

you will need:

4 oz. short pastry (see page 64)	little water
1 lb. cooking apples	2 oz. butter or margarine
4 oz. brown sugar	2 yolks of egg
For the meringue topping:	
2 egg whites	4 oz. castor sugar

1 Line a tart tin or shallow ovenware dish with the pastry; mark the edges with a fork or spoon.
2 Stew the apples with the brown sugar, a little water to prevent sticking, and the butter or margarine, until apples become pulpy.
3 Rub through a sieve or beat until apples are quite smooth.
4 Add the beaten egg yolks and mix well.
5 Pour into the prepared tart tin or dish. Bake until pastry is brown and apple mixture firm, in moderate oven. Cool slightly.
6 Whip the egg whites till stiff; add half the castor sugar, a teaspoon at a time.
7 Continue whisking until stiff and dry, then fold in remaining sugar.

8 Spread over the apple mixture in tart tin, piling it up and taking it right up to the edge of the pastry.
9 Return to moderate oven until meringue is pale brown and set.

Blackberry and Apple Pie

you will need:

8 oz. short pastry (see page 64)	8–12 oz. apples 4 oz. brown sugar
12 oz. to 1 lb. blackberries	

1 Roll out pastry thinly, and put a 1-inch strip around the wetted edge of a deep pie dish.
2 Put a pie funnel or egg cup in middle of dish, and fill with the washed berries and the peeled, cored and sliced apples, sprinkling the sugar among the fruit.
3 Dampen pastry edge; put a lid of pastry over the fruit, trim off the edges, press well and mark with a fork.
4 Make a small hole in the middle and bake in a hot oven (425°F.—Gas Mark 7) for 20 minutes to allow pastry to set, then lower heat to 380°F.—Gas Mark 5, and cook a further 15–20 minutes, to finish cooking fruit.
   Serve with Custard Sauce (see page 70).
   Sprinkle top with castor sugar.

Strawberry-Rhubarb Cream Flan

you will need

8 oz. red rhubarb	1 pint milk
1½ tablespoons sugar	1 tablespoon sugar
1 packet strawberry flavoured jelly	few fresh or frozen whole strawberries
1 packet strawberry flavoured cornflour or blancmange	8-inch short or biscuit pastry case

1 Wipe rhubarb, cut it into ½-inch pieces, cook until soft with a little water and 1½ tablespoons sugar.
2 Rub through a sieve; there should be about ½ pint purée.
3 Dissolve the jelly in ¾ pint water; add half of it to the rhubarb purée.
4 Make up the flavoured cornflour with the milk and sugar; allow to cool a little then mix with the rhubarb/strawberry mixture. Pour into the pastry case.
5 Leave to go quite cold, then pour remaining liquid jelly over the top.
6 Decorate with a few fresh or frozen whole strawberries.

Note:
There may be too much filling for the pastry case, but the surplus can be kept to serve with custard, or to fill small tartlet cases. These small cases are baked in the same way as the large pastry cases; with a circle of bread inside to prevent pastry rising. It is not necessary to line with paper.

Windermere Tart

you will need:

6 oz. short pastry (see page 64)	2 tablespoons strawberry jam
½-pint measure young rhubarb, cut up	1 tablespoon castor sugar
	few marshmallows

1 Roll out pastry and line a 7–8-inch sandwich cake tin with it, avoiding stretching the pastry.
2 Press the pastry down well, and around edges of tin; prick bottom and sides and press again to expel air.
3 Trim the edges, roll out pieces and cut six narrow strips from it, long enough to go over top of tin.
4 Mix the rhubarb and jam, adding sugar. Put into the pastry-lined tin, spreading it evenly.
5 Place the strips of pastry in a lattice pattern across top of tart, moistening the ends so they stick securely to rim of tart.
6 Bake in fairly hot oven (400°F.—Gas Mark 6) 20 to 25 minutes.
7 When the tart is almost done (pastry just turning light brown) place a marshmallow in each space made by pastry strips, and return to oven for a few minutes for pastry to finish browning and for the marshmallows to become just tipped with brown.
As an alternative to the marshmallows: if you have a spare egg white, this can be whipped until white and fluffy, adding a teaspoonful castor sugar. Then put a teaspoon of the mixture in each square and return tart to oven for final browning.

Strawberry Meringue Pie

you will need:

8 oz. strawberries	2 egg yolks
2 heaped teaspoons strawberry flavoured cornflour or blancmange	pastry case made with Biscuit Crust (see page 65), using 6 oz. flour, 3 oz. margarine
¼ pint water	
squeeze of lemon juice	
For the Meringue Topping:	
2 egg whites	2 oz. castor sugar

1 Reserve a few perfect berries; beat remainder to a smooth pulp with fork.
2 Blend cornflour or blancmange to a smooth paste with a little water, boil the water and pour over the paste, add lemon juice, put in pan and bring to boil, stirring.
3 Simmer 2–3 minutes, cool slightly then add the beaten egg yolks.
4 Mix well, then add the strawberry purée, and beat again.
5 Put mixture into pastry case; pile the meringue on top spreading it well out to the sides and piling slightly in the middle; mark in whirls with fork.
6 Place in hot oven for a few minutes (425°F.—Gas Mark 7) until meringue sets and is tipped with brown. Garnish with a few perfect berries.

Note:
This pie is best eaten straight from the oven while the meringue topping is crisp; it can be left for one day and eaten cold, but if left longer the topping becomes 'tacky'. It must be remembered that this is a meringue *topping*, not to be confused with *meringues* which are dried out in an oven for hours until they are crisp all through and will stay that way indefinitely.

Strawberry Tartlets

you will need:

½ pint liquid strawberry jelly	1 whipped egg white *with* teaspoon castor added
8–12 oz. strawberries (small ones are best)	
1 dozen tartlet cases (see this page), made from 6 oz. flour and 3 oz. margarine	

1 Make the liquid jelly from packet of jelly squares, leave to go cold but not set.
2 Stalk the strawberries, clean them in a towel (avoid washing). Pick out 6 perfect ones.
3 Arrange 3 to 4 strawberries (according to size) in the tartlet cases.
4 When jelly is cool, spoon it over the berries, so they are thinly coated with it. Leave for jelly to set.
5 Just before serving put small blobs of whipped egg white on top of the tartlets.
6 Cut the remaining 6 berries into halves and place them, cut sides downwards on top of the egg white.
Stoned Cherries may be used in the same way; red or black cherries are best. Whitehearts are not juicy enough. Use any flavour of red-coloured jelly.

Macaroni Fruit Pudding

you will need:

6 oz. short cut macaroni	2 oz. currants
1 pint water	2 oz. sultanas
1 teaspoon salt	1 oz. butter
1 pint milk	grated nutmeg
1 egg	
2 tablespoons golden syrup	

1 Boil the macaroni in the water with salt added 5–7 minutes. Drain and return to pan.
2 Add the milk, bring to the boil, stirring all the time. Remove from heat, stir in beaten egg and the syrup.
3 Add the cleaned fruit and the butter, mix well.
4 Pour into a buttered pie-dish, grate nutmeg over. Bake in moderate oven (355°F.—Gas Mark 5) for 30 minutes.

Bilberry Tapioca

you will need:

2 oz. fine tapioca	1 large or 2 small eggs
½ pint water	12 oz. bilberries
4 oz. castor sugar	

1 Boil the tapioca in the water, with pinch of salt added until it is clear and jellified. Stir well.
2 Add half the sugar and the yolk of egg and whip well, away from heat.
3 Clean the bilberries and put them in a glass heatproof pudding dish; sprinkle remaining sugar over them, reserving 1 tablespoon.
4 Pour the tapioca over the berries and bake in moderate oven (355°F.—Gas Mark 4) for 20 minutes.
5 Whip the egg white until stiff, gradually adding the remaining sugar.
6 Spread this meringue topping over the tapioca and return to upper shelf of oven until lightly browned. Serve at once.

Fresh Apricot Pudding

you will need:

1 oz. butter	4 oz. shredded suet
8 oz. fresh apricots	2 tablespoons granulated sugar
4 oz. self-raising flour	2 eggs
4 oz. fine white bread-crumbs	little milk to mix
salt	2 teaspoons Demerara sugar

1 Well butter a 2-pint pudding basin; line bottom and sides with stoned and halved apricots, placing skin sides next to basin.
2 Mix flour and breadcrumbs, adding pinch salt, then add suet and sugar and mix thoroughly.
3 Stir in the beaten eggs with a little milk, and stir well until eggs are evenly blended. Add a little more milk to make a stiffly dropping consistency.
4 Sprinkle Demerara sugar over the apricots in the basin, add butter in pieces, then put in the pudding mixture, smoothing the top.
5 Cover with buttered paper, tied on tightly, but loosely fitting to allow pudding to rise. Simmer gently for 2 hours.
6 Turn out carefully, to disturb apricots as little as possible and serve with Apricot Sauce.

Apricot Sauce

you will need:

8 fresh apricots	1 tablespoon apricot jam
½ pint water	2 teaspoons cornflour
3 teaspoons Demerara sugar	

1 Chop apricots into quarters; crack stones and remove kernels.
2 Cook apricots and stones in the water and sugar for 10 minutes or until soft. Add the jam.
3 Blend cornflour to a smooth paste with a tablespoon of water, add to boiling apricot mixture, stir until boiling again and mixture clears and thickens slightly. Pour into a sauce boat to serve.

Quick Orange Dessert

you will need:

2 large Jaffa oranges, halved	1 oz. butter
4 oz. milk chocolate biscuits	4 glacé cherries

1 Cut a thin slice off the bottoms of the orange halves so that they stand steady. Scoop out the pulp; remove as much inner skin as possible from the pulp.
2 Crush the biscuits to fine crumbs; mix with the pulp.
3 Stuff the half orange shells with the mixture, piling it well up. Dot with butter, and stand on a fireproof plate.
4 Place low down under red-hot grill until heated through and the tops are crisp.
5 Serve with a glacé cherry on top of each.

Apricot-Walnut Sponge

you will need:

3 tablespoons apricot jam	1 tablespoon cold water
3 oz. butter	1½ oz. finely chopped
3 oz. castor sugar	walnuts
2 eggs	½ oz. walnut halves for
4 oz. self-raising flour	decoration

1 Butter a 1½- or 2-pint pudding basin and cover the bottom with 2 tablespoons of the jam.
2 Cream the butter and sugar until light, beat in the eggs, then fold in the flour.
3 Add the water and beat lightly, then fold in the chopped nuts.
4 Pour into the pudding basin (it should be two-thirds full). Cover with greaseproof paper or foil, making a pleat in the top to allow for pudding rising.
5 Place in pan with boiling water to come half-way up the basin; simmer gently 1¼ to 1½ hours.
6 Turn out on to hot dish, coat with remaining jam and arrange walnut halves around top. Or remaining jam may be heated with a little water and served as sauce.

Crumbly-Crust Pies

Basic Crumb Crust

you will need:

6 oz. plain flour	2 oz. castor sugar
¼ teaspoon salt	
3 oz. butter or best margarine	

1 Sieve flour and salt into bowl.
2 Rub in fat with finger-tips until mixture resembles breadcrumbs.
3 Add sugar, and mix well with a fork.
Pastry is now ready for use; no water is added. If not needed at once it can be stored in air-tight jar or polythene bag in fridge or cold place. Sugar is omitted if crust is used for savoury pies. Cake and biscuit crumbs, crushed cornflakes, quick-cooking oats, fine bread-crumbs, can all be used for crumbly toppings.

Spiced Crumb Crust: Add ¼ teaspoon mixed cake spice to the flour. Powdered cinnamon, nutmeg, or ground cloves may be used. Good for apple pies.
Pea-nut Butter Crust: Use half pea-nut butter and half ordinary butter or margarine.
Almond Crumb Crust: Use 2 oz. ground almonds and 4 oz. flour instead of 6 oz. flour, and only 2 oz. fat as almonds are oily.
Chocolate Crumb Crust: Add a dessertspoon sweetened chocolate powder to the flour.
Coffee Crumb Crust: Add a heaped teaspoon instant coffee powder to the flour.
Cereal, Biscuit, or Cake-Crumb Crust: Substitute any of these for the flour in the same proportion, but melt the fat to mix it in. Sweet cake and biscuit crumbs do not need sugar; stale cake is better than fresh.

Fruit Pies with Crumbly Crust
Almost any fruit in season, or tinned, bottled or frozen fruit can be used. Add as little juice or water as possible – none at all for very juicy fruits such as raspberries or loganberries or blackberries – as the moisture would soak into the crust and it would not be crisp as it should be.
Put the fruit, cut up if need be, in a well-buttered shallow pie dish, cover with the crumb crust, pressing it well down. Bake in fairly hot oven (400°F.—Gas Mark 6) for 20 to 30 minutes, according to the fruit used.

Toffee Crust Apple Pie

you will need:

4 oz. plain flour	2 oz. granulated sugar
6 oz. soft brown sugar	½ teaspoon powdered
3 oz. butter or best margarine	cinnamon
1 lb. cooking apples	4 tablespoons water

1 Mix flour and sugar, add fat and mix with finger-tips until crumbly.
2 Peel and core apples and cut into wedges about ¼ inch thick.
3 Well butter a pie dish, 1½ inches deep, 7 to 8 inches across.
4 Put in the apples, spreading them evenly, sprinkle with granulated sugar and cinnamon; sprinkle water over.
5 Cover with the toffee crumbly crust, pressing it well down.
6 Bake in moderate oven, (375°F.—Gas Mark 5), until crust is well browned, with a toffee-like finish – 25 to 30 minutes. Serve hot.

Fruit, Jelly and Custard Desserts

Pouring Custard

you will need:

½ pint milk
2 egg yolks
1 heaped teaspoon
    castor sugar

3 drops vanilla essence

1 Heat the milk, and pour over the beaten egg yolks.
2 Strain back into pan, add sugar, stir until custard thickens and remove instantly; do not boil. Add vanilla.
3 Serve hot or cold as a sauce for stewed fruit, fruit pies or tarts, or cold with jellies.
The custard may be flavoured with *lemon rind*, which is put into the milk while heating it.
If liked, the whites of the eggs can be whipped stiffly and added when the sauce has cooled a little. They should be *folded* in, not beaten.
But *egg whites left over* after yolks are used come in very useful for making meringues, which can be served as a light pudding or for teatime, or they can be reserved to use for meringue topping for flans, etc.
Egg whites will keep for several days in a covered container, in the fridge.

For **Coffee Pouring Custard** use ¼ pint strong coffee (may be made with instant coffee powder) and ¼ pint milk.

Vanilla Cream

you will need:

1 pint milk
2 eggs
1 tablespoon sugar
1 teaspoon vanilla
    essence

½ oz. gelatine
2 tablespoons water
2 tablespoons cream
    from top of milk, or
    evaporated milk

1 Heat the milk. Beat eggs, sugar and vanilla together.
2 Pour the warm milk over egg mixture; return to pan and stir until it thickens sufficiently to coat back of spoon.
3 Pour at once into a cold basin, leave to cool, stirring occasionally.
4 Dissolve gelatine in the water over low heat.
5 While still hot pour into the custard; add the cream or evaporated milk and whip well.
6 When the mixture begins to thicken, pour into a fancy mould, leave to set, then turn out on to a plate.

Note:
The mould can be decorated with glacé fruits, such as glacé cherries and strips of angelica, or chopped jelly looks very pretty around the base. The mould can be previously decorated with a layer of jelly, which must be set before the vanilla cream is poured in.
If liked the vanilla cream can be poured into individual moulds, or small glass dishes; in the latter case there is no need to turn them out. Decorate tops with fruits or mask with a layer of jelly.

Honeycomb Mould

you will need:

1 pint milk
2 eggs
1 oz. sugar
½ oz. gelatine

1 tablespoon water
1 teaspoon vanilla
    essence

1 Put the milk in top of double boiler, or in basin standing in boiling water.
2 Separate eggs, beat yolks, add to milk with sugar.
3 Cook over low heat, water simmering in bottom of double boiler or in pan. Stir until mixture begins to thicken.
4 Dissolve gelatine in tablespoon water over heat and add to custard in pan; stir until mixture thickens.
5 Remove from heat. Beat egg whites to stiff froth. Fold these into the cooled mixture, gradually adding the vanilla essence. Pour into mould, rinsed out with cold water.
6 When cold turn out into a glass dish; decorate with fresh fruit in season, or bottled fruit, around base of mould.
Alternative Flavourings: Lemon or orange rind which should be infused in milk; use orange or lemon juice to taste instead of vanilla.
A teaspoon of strong coffee essence instead of the vanilla, or ¼ pint strong coffee and ¾ pint milk.

Prune Mould

you will need:

8 oz. prunes
½ pint water
2 oz. sugar
grated rind and juice of
    1 lemon

1 inch cinnamon
½ oz. gelatine
few blanched, split
    almonds
1 tablespoon red jam

1 Wash and soak prunes in the water, overnight.
2 Put soaked prunes in pan with half the water, sugar, lemon rind and cinnamon.
3 Cook until tender, remove cinnamon, then stone the prunes, chop them finely or sieve.
4 Dissolve the gelatine in the remaining $\frac{1}{4}$ pint water. Chop two or three almonds finely.
5 Add the lemon juice, jam, gelatine and chopped almonds to the sieved prunes; make up to 1 pint with water, if necessary.
6 Stir thoroughly until almost cold, then pour into a mould.
7 When set, turn out into glass dish; decorate top and sides with blanched almonds cut into thin strips.
8 Serve with a cold, pouring custard sauce (see page 70).

Apple Snow

you will need:

2 small sponge cakes or stale sponge sandwich cake	3 oz. castor sugar juice of 1 lemon 1 egg white
$\frac{1}{4}$ pint pouring custard (see page 70)	glacé fruit, fresh or canned fruit to decorate
4 oz. cooking apples, stewed and sieved	

1 Cut sponge cakes into thin slices, spread them in the bottom of glass dish.
2 Pour the custard over, and leave to set.
3 Put apple pulp in basin, add sugar and lemon juice.
4 Whisk egg white until stiff, add to the apple, and whip until mixture is quite stiff and fluffy.
5 Pile it on to the custard, and serve at once, decorated with glacé cherries, fresh berry fruit, or canned fruit.
Note:
If using canned fruit, some of the juice can be added to the water for stewing the apples.
If you can't spare an egg, the Apple Snow can be made with a $\frac{1}{2}$ pint packet jelly, made up with $\frac{1}{4}$ pint water. This must cool, and when it is beginning to thicken, whisk it into the apple pulp.

Raspberry Chiffon

you will need:

1 pint raspberry jelly square	2 tablespoons castor sugar
$\frac{1}{2}$ pint boiling water	1 egg white
1 lb. raspberries	
3 tablespoons hot water	

1 Dissolve the jelly in the boiling water.
2 Pick over the raspberries, wiping them with a soft cloth if necessary (avoid washing). Reserve a dozen or so perfect ones for decoration.
3 Put remainder in pan with 3 tablespoons hot water and the sugar.
4 Bring slowly to the boil, remove immediately; rub through sieve.
5 When raspberry jelly is on the point of setting, whisk it until frothy, using wire egg whisk.
6 Add raspberry purée and whip again until mixture begins to stiffen.
7 Whisk egg white until stiff, fold it gently into raspberry mixture.
8 Pile into individual dishes; arrange the reserved raspberries on top.
Note:
It is better not to put the Raspberry Chiffon into a large glass dish, as it is so light it will 'fall' as soon as the spoon is put in for serving. Strawberries, blackcurrants, redcurrants, bilberries, gooseberries – any fruit that will reduce to a pulp – may be used, varying the flavour of the jelly accordingly.

Raspberry Trifle

you will need:

4 small sponge cakes or 4 oz. stale sponge cake	1 pint milk
little raspberry jam	1 tablespoon sugar
12 oz. fresh or frozen raspberries	$\frac{1}{3}$ pint whipped cream or evaporated milk
1 raspberry jelly square	few strips angelica, and blanched almonds for decoration
1 pint packet raspberry cornflour	

1 Slice the cakes and sandwich them together with jam; place in glass dish.
2 Thaw the raspberries if frozen; add any syrup to boiling water to make up to a pint; dissolve jelly in this.
3 Pour liquid jelly over sponge cakes, reserving a little to set for decoration.
4 When jelly has soaked into the sponge cake, spread a layer of raspberries on top; keep back a few perfect ones to decorate top of trifle. Leave to set.
5 Make the raspberry cornflour up with the milk and sugar. Leave to cool, but not stiffen, stirring occasionally.
6 Pour over the sponge cake and jelly in dish; spread smoothly.
7 Whip the cream or evaporated milk. When raspberry custard is quite cold and stiffened spread the cream on top.
8 Decorate with chopped jelly, and raspberries, making stalks of angelica, and sprinkle chopped almonds over.

Strawberry Orange Mousse

you will need:

1 can strawberries (8 oz.)	½ large can (6½ fl. oz.)
1 packet orange jelly	evaporated milk
1 tablespoon concentrated orange squash	

1 Drain strawberries and dissolve the jelly in the juice over low heat.
2 Rub strawberries through sieve, add to the jelly with the orange squash and allow to cool until almost setting.
3 Chill evaporated milk and whisk until thick.
4 Slowly add fruit jelly and whisk until almost set.
5 Pour into individual fruit dishes.

Pineapple Mousse (see front cover)

you will need:

1 can pineapple chunks (13½ oz.)	½ large can (6½ fl. oz.) evaporated milk
1 packet pineapple jelly	glacé cherries and
1 teaspoon lemon juice	angelica

1 Drain pineapple and dissolve jelly in the juice over low heat.
2 Reserve a few pieces of pineapple for decoration. Chop or liquidise remainder, and add to jelly with the lemon juice.
3 Allow to cool until almost setting.
4 Chill evaporated milk and whisk until thick.
5 Slowly add fruit jelly and whisk until almost set.
6 Pour into individual fruit dishes.
7 When set decorate, using reserved pieces of pineapple, glacé cherries and angelica.

Sago and Rhubarb Mould

you will need:

1 lb. young rhubarb	3 oz. fine sago
½ pint water	red colouring if
2 oz. sugar	necessary
grated rind ½ lemon	

1 Wipe rhubarb, cut it into small pieces, and stew with the water, sugar and lemon rind.
2 When rhubarb is tender, sprinkle in the sago. Cook until sago is clear, stirring all the time.
3 Add a few drops red colouring to give a good pink.
4 Pour into a mould; when set, turn out and serve with Pouring Custard Sauce (see page 70).

Quick cooking tapioca may be used; also semolina, but the mould will not be so clear as when sago or tapioca is used.

Pear Condé

you will need:

4 eating pears	1 oz. butter
2 oz. sugar	1 teaspoon cornflour
4 oz. best rice	few drops red colouring
1 pint milk	
few drops vanilla essence	

1 Peel pears, cut in halves, remove cores.
2 Just cover with water with a little sugar added, and simmer gently until soft. Leave pears in their syrup to go cold.
3 Wash rice, place in cold water, bring to the boil, drain, and rinse in cold water.
4 Place in saucepan with milk and sugar, cook slowly until rice is cooked, but not mushy. Drain.
5 Add the essence, and the butter; leave to go cold.
6 Arrange the rice in a heap on serving dish, and stand the pear halves all round.
7 Add a tablespoon sugar to ¼ pint of the syrup in which pears were cooked, boil for a few minutes, add cornflour blended with a little juice.
8 Boil up again until sauce thickens slightly and clears. Add a few drops red colouring. Cool, then pour over pears.

Plain Macaroni Milk Pudding

you will need:

3 oz. short cut macaroni	1 oz. sugar
1 pint milk	grated nutmeg
pinch salt	

1 Butter a rice pudding dish, put in the macaroni, milk and salt. Stir and leave to soak ¾ to 1 hour.
2 Add sugar and stir well.
3 Bake in fairly slow oven (350°F.—Gas Mark 4) for 45 minutes to 1 hour.
4 Stir the pudding after cooking 25 minutes, grate nutmeg over top and cook until macaroni is soft and top well browned.
5 Serve hot or cold, with stewed fruit or jam sauce (page 64).
This pudding can be varied by the addition of flavouring essences, currants, sultanas or chopped dates.
An egg can be beaten into the milk for extra richness.
The fancy shaped macaroni (shells, wheels, etc.) can be used instead of plain short cut macaroni.

Cakes, Buns and Biscuits

Cut-and-Come-Again Cake

you will need:

1 lb. self-raising flour	4 oz. chopped candied
6 oz. soft brown sugar	peel
(Barbados)	6 oz. best margarine
¼ teaspoon salt	3 eggs
2 rounded teaspoons	about 4 tablespoons
mixed cake spice	milk
12 oz. mixed dried fruits	
(equal quantities currants,	
raisins, sultanas)	

1 Sieve flour, sugar, salt, spice into mixing bowl. Add fruit and peel and mix well.
2 Chop the margarine roughly (about 6 pieces), add to dry mixture and mix with a spoon, pressing margarine against sides of bowl until it is well coated with flour.
3 Add the beaten eggs, and enough milk to give a stiff dropping consistency.
4 Put the mixture in a greased and paper-lined 7–8-inch cake tin; smooth top evenly.
5 Bake in moderate oven (355°F.—Gas Mark 4) for 1 to 1¼ hours. Turn out and cool on wire tray.

Note:
With modern quickly melting margarines it is not necessary to rub in with the fingers.
It saves time if you use ready-cleaned packaged fruit and ready-cut candied peel.
For **Rock Buns**, put the mixture in rough piles on a greased oven sheet, using two forks. Bake 15 to 20 minutes.

Chocolate Cake

you will need:

6 oz. self-raising flour	3 oz. sugar
2 oz. sweetened chocolate	2 eggs
powder	1 tablespoon golden syrup
pinch salt	little milk, if necessary
4 oz. butter or best	
margarine	

1 Sieve flour, chocolate powder and salt into bowl.
2 Cream fat and sugar together until light; beat eggs well.
3 Add eggs and dry mixture alternately to the creamed fat and sugar, beating well.
4 After all flour is added, add the melted syrup, and milk if necessary to make a soft dropping consistency.

5 Pour into a greased and lined tin 7 inches by 3 inches deep, smoothing the top.
6 Bake in middle of fairly hot oven (400°F.—Gas Mark 6) 1–1¼ hours. Cool in tin before turning out on wire tray.

Note:
The use of golden syrup means that you use 1 oz. less of sugar, and very little milk; if golden syrup is omitted, use 4 oz. sugar and little more milk. But the use of golden syrup gives a moister texture to the cake.
For **Chocolate Buns:** Brush inside bun tins with melted fat; half-fill tins with cake mixture; bake 20 to 25 minutes.

Family Gingerbread

you will need:

12 oz. plain flour	4 tablespoons milk
¼ teaspoon salt	6 oz. golden syrup
½ oz. ground ginger	2 oz. dark treacle
1 rounded teaspoon mixed	5 oz. lard and margarine
cake spice	mixed
1 rounded teaspoon	3 eggs
ground cinnamon	1 rounded teaspoon
3 oz. soft brown sugar	bicarbonate soda

1 Grease and paper-line an oblong Yorkshire pudding tin about 10 inches long by 7 inches wide and 2½ inches deep.
2 Sieve together flour, salt and spices; add sugar; mix well.
2 Heat 3 tablespoons milk, syrup, treacle and fats in a saucepan until fats melt.
4 Add beaten eggs to dry mixture, then beat in fats, treacle and milk mixture.
5 Dissolve bicarbonate soda in remaining milk, slightly warmed; beat this into mixture.
6 Pour into prepared tin, spreading it evenly.
7 Bake on middle shelf of moderate oven (375°F. —Gas Mark 5), for 50 minutes, or until well risen and spongy to the touch.
8 Cool in tin; cut into squares when quite cold.

Note:
Gingerbread should be kept in a tin to keep it moist.
For **Ginger Buns:** half-fill greased bun tins with the mixture; bake 12 to 15 minutes.

Dripping Cake

you will need:

8 oz. mixed dried fruit (include candied peel)
4 oz. clarified beef or pork dripping
4 oz. soft brown sugar
1 tablespoon treacle
¼ pint water

4 oz. wholemeal flour
4 oz. self raising flour
¼ teaspoon salt
1 teaspoon mixed cake spice
½ teaspoon bicarbonate soda

1 Put the cleaned fruit with the dripping, sugar, treacle and water in a saucepan and simmer 5 minutes.
2 Sieve flours with salt and spice and mix gradually into the cooled mixture; stir well.
3 Add bicarbonate soda dissolved in a teaspoon warm water.
4 Turn into a well-greased 1-lb. loaf tin. Bake in moderate oven (355°F.—Gas Mark 4) for 1¼ to 1½ hours.

Note:

As this is an eggless cake, it will not rise much; it should be eaten fairly quickly.

To **clarify dripping:** Place it in a pan with ¼ pint water, bring to the boil, then pour it into a basin. Leave until dripping sets, then remove it in a 'cake' and scrape off sediment on underside. Put dripping in pan, heat to boiling point, pour off and leave to set before using. Mutton dripping should not be used for cake making.

Sponge Sandwich (Victoria Sponge)

you will need:

6 oz. self-raising flour
pinch of salt
6 oz. butter or best margarine

6 oz. castor sugar
2 large eggs, or 3 small
1–2 tablespoons milk
few drops vanilla essence

1 Sieve flour with pinch salt.
2 Cream together fat and sugar until light and creamy colour.
3 Add the eggs one at a time, beating well, and sprinkling in a little flour between each egg.
4 Beat well after the addition of last egg, then gently fold in remaining flour with a metal spoon; do not beat again.
5 Add milk as necessary to make a stiffly flowing consistency; add the essence last.
6 Pour the mixture into two well-greased and floured 7½ to 8-inch sandwich tins, allowing the mixture to settle smoothly in the tins.

7 Bake side by side on the middle shelf of moderate oven (355°F.—Gas Mark 4) for 20 to 25 minutes.
8 When done, leave to cool slightly in tins, then turn out on to wire tray. When cold sandwich together with jam or lemon curd, or cream filling.

For **Cream Filling:** 2 oz. butter or best margarine, 4 oz. sieved icing sugar, ½ tablespoon milk. Put all in mixing bowl and cream until light and fluffy.

For **Coffee Filling:** use ½ tablespoon coffee essence in place of milk.

Swiss Roll

you will need:

3 oz. plain flour
1 teaspoon baking powder
pinch salt
2 eggs

3 oz. castor sugar
1 tablespoon warm water
8 oz. raspberry or strawberry jam

1 Sieve flour, salt and baking powder twice.
2 Beat eggs well in mixing bowl; add sugar and beat with rotary beater or wire whisk 5 minutes.
3 Lightly fold in flour, etc., with metal spoon or palette knife.
4 Stir gently until smooth, gradually adding the warm water; do not beat.
5 Oil an 11½ inches by 7½ inches sandwich tin with melted butter or oil.
6 Line tin with greaseproof paper to extend an inch above rim; brush this with butter or oil.
7 Pour in the sponge mixture, spreading it evenly.
8 Bake centre of fairly hot oven (400°F.—Gas Mark 6) 12 to 15 minutes. The cake should be an even golden brown and springy to the touch.
9 When sponge is baked, invert tin over a dampened, sugar sprinkled towel, and carefully remove paper.
10 Cut a ½-inch strip from the edges of sponge, and make a short cut inwards each side 2 inches from end.
11 Spread warmed jam to within ¼ inch of edges; fold over at split end and press firmly, then bring the sugared cloth up and with fingers under the cloth roll the sponge over and over away from you.
12 Hold in position for a minute or so, still covered with the cloth, to allow the roll to 'set'.
13 Remove the cloth and lift carefully on to wire tray and leave until cold.

Cream-Filled Swiss Roll: After turning out the sponge on to sugared cloth, cover it with a sheet of greaseproof paper (first removing strips from side and making slit near one end) and roll up. Leave until cold, then carefully unroll, remove paper and spread with Mock Cream (see page 79), and roll up again.

Chocolate Swiss Roll: Remove 2 tablespoons flour and replace with 2 level tablespoons sweetened chocolate powder; bake and proceed as for Cream-filled Swiss Roll.

Basic Bun Mixture

you will need:

8 oz. plain flour	1½ teaspoons baking
good pinch salt	powder
4 oz. butter or best	1 large egg
margarine	2 tablespoons milk
4 oz. castor sugar	

1 Sieve flour and salt into basin.
2 Rub fat in until crumbly.
3 Add sugar and baking powder.
4 Mix with egg and milk until mixture is stiff enough for fork to stand upright in it.
5 Place the mixture in small rocky heaps on greased baking sheet, using two forks; place them well apart.
6 Bake in hot oven (425°F.—Gas Mark 7) for 12 to 15 minutes, until lightly browned.

The mixture may be flavoured with a few drops of Vanilla Essence or Almond Essence added at the end.

For **Coconut Buns:** Add 2–3 oz. desiccated coconut to the flour.

Lemon Buns: Add grated rind ½ lemon, and the juice, using less milk.

Caraway Buns: Add a dessertspoon caraway seeds to the sugar before adding it to the flour.

Raspberry Buns: Flatten heaps slightly, make small hollow in each. Fill hollows with raspberry jam and draw the mixture over it; sprinkle with castor sugar.

Sour Milk Scones

you will need:

8 oz. plain flour	1 teaspoon golden syrup
1 teaspoon baking powder	¼ pint sour milk
½ teaspoon salt	

1 Mix all dry ingredients thoroughly.
2 Warm the syrup; add to the sour milk.
3 Stir into the flour, etc., until a pliable dough is formed.
4 Knead lightly on floured board until quite smooth.
5 Roll out about ¼ inch thick; cut into rounds.
6 Bake on a hot greased girdle or thick frying pan until well risen and browned on both sides.
7 Cover with clean towel to cool, then serve at once, split, with butter, or butter and jam inside.

Note:
The whole ¼ pint sour milk may not be needed, as it is inclined to liquify in mixing; be careful not to get the mixture too soft.
Do not cut the scones with a knife; make a slight incision and gently tear them open.

Dropped Scones

you will need:

8 oz. flour	1 oz. lard
1 teaspoon baking powder	1 egg
¼ teaspoon salt	2–3 tablespoons sour milk
1 heaped tablespoon castor sugar	

1 Mix all the dry ingredients thoroughly.
2 Rub in the lard.
3 Beat in the egg; add milk until mixture is a fairly soft, flowing consistency; beat well.
4 Heat a girdle or thick frying pan; rub it over with soft paper dipped in oil or melted butter.
5 Drop dessertspoons of the mixture on the hot surface, spacing well apart.
6 Cook until brown underneath and bubbly on top; turn and brown underside.
7 Cool slightly on tea-cloth; spread with butter and serve at once.
Grease the girdle or frying pan afresh for each lot of scones.

Madeira Cake

you will need:

8 oz. self-raising flour	grated rind of lemon
3 eggs	milk if necessary
4 oz. butter or best margarine	citron peel for top (optional)
6 oz. castor sugar	

1 Sieve the flour. Beat the eggs well.
2 Cream fat and sugar until light, in mixing bowl.
3 Add beaten egg and flour alternately to the creamed fat and sugar. After last flour is added beat a further 2–3 minutes.
4 Add the lemon rind, and mix gently, with milk if necessary to make a mixture that drops softly from the spoon.
5 Put into greased and lined 7-inch cake tin; bake in middle of fairly hot oven (380°F.—Gas Mark 5), 1 hour to 1 hour 10 minutes.
6 After about 20 minutes' baking, when cake is beginning to set, put a piece of citron peel on top. Close oven door quickly and complete baking.

For **Cherry Madeira Cake:** Add 4 oz. glacé cherries to the mixture after the flour has been added. The cherries should first be rinsed to remove surplus sugar, then dried and cut into quarters. Omit the citron peel on top, and instead arrange a few cherries cut in halves after the cake is baked.

Cornflour Cake: Use 4 oz. flour and 4 oz. cornflour. Add a few drops vanilla essence.

Ground Rice Cake: Use 4 oz. flour and 4 oz. ground rice; flavour with ¼ teaspoon grated nutmeg.

Seed Cake: Add 1 level tablespoon caraway seeds and ½ teaspoon powdered cinnamon.

Queen Cakes: Add 4 oz. cleaned currants; bake in Queen Cake tins, or paper cases in moderate oven 15–20 minutes.

Sultana Cake: Add 6–8 oz. sultanas or seedless raisins and a few drops vanilla essence.

Coffee Cake: Mix to required consistency using 1 to 1½ tablespoons coffee essence or strong black coffee.

Walnut Cake: Add 3 oz. chopped walnuts and 1 teaspoon vanilla essence. Ice with American Icing (see page 79), and decorate with walnut halves.

Nut and Cherry Tea Bread

you will need:

12 oz. self-raising flour	½ pint milk (less 1 tablespoon)
¼ teaspoon salt	1 large egg
3 oz. castor sugar	2 oz. melted butter or margarine
2 oz. flaked almonds or chopped walnuts	
3 oz. halved glacé cherries	

1 Mix flour, salt, sugar in basin.
2 Reserve a few cherries and nuts for top of cake then add rest to flour mixture.
3 Mix to a fairly stiff consistency with milk and egg, then stir in melted fat.
4 Turn mixture into a greased 1-lb. loaf tin.
5 Smooth top and sprinkle with reserved nuts and arrange cherries down centre.
6 Bake in moderate oven (355°F.—Gas Mark 4) 1 to 1¼ hours. Cool on wire tray and leave overnight.
7 Serve sliced and buttered.

Note:
There may be too much mixture for the tin; in this case put the extra into bun tins and bake 12 to 15 minutes.

Currants and Raisins may be used instead of cherries.

Grumble Cake (Uncooked)

you will need:

8 oz. plain broken biscuits	1 tablespoon sweetened chocolate powder
2 oz. margarine or butter	2 oz. chopped raisins and dates
1 oz. sugar	
1 tablespoon golden syrup	

1 Crush the biscuits with rolling pin.
2 Melt the margarine, syrup and sugar together in mixing bowl.
3 Add the chocolate powder and the biscuits, mix well, then add the fruit and stir well together.
4 Grease a loose-bottomed 6-7-inch cake tin, press the mixture into it.
5 Leave overnight in fridge if possible.
6 Turn out by pushing up the loose bottom of cake tin; cut in pieces for serving.

Note:
Chocolate polka dots may be used instead of chopped fruit, and a few nuts may be added. If sufficient biscuits are not available, make up with stale cake crumbs; it is important that the mixture should not be too soft, therefore moist cake should not be used.

Flapjacks

you will need:

4 oz. butter or best margarine
1 oz. soft brown sugar
2 tablespoons golden syrup

8 oz. quick-cook rolled oats
½ teaspoon salt

1 Melt the fat, sugar, syrup in saucepan over low heat.
2 Work in the oats and salt.
3 Cool slightly then press into a greased Swiss roll tin, or Yorkshire pudding tin.
4 Bake in moderate oven (355°F.—Gas Mark 4) for 30 to 40 minutes.
5 Leave in the baking tin for a few minutes.
6 Before it gets hard, cut into oblongs; leave in the tin until cold, then store in cake tin.

Note:
The flapjacks will be crisp when first baked, but will become 'tacky' if left a day or two; some people prefer them that way.

Chocolate-Nutty Crisps

you will need:

4 oz. plain chocolate
2 oz. chopped almonds or walnuts

2 oz. crispy rice or corn cereal

1 Break chocolate into small pieces; melt it in a bowl over hot water.
2 Add the chopped nuts, mix well, add the cereal and stir until evenly blended. Mixture will be very stiff.
3 Put teaspoon of mixture in waxed paper small cake cases; do not smooth the tops.
4 Put in fridge or cold place to harden.
A few raisins or currants may be added, using less cereal, accordingly.

Meringues

you will need:

egg whites
2 oz. castor sugar to each egg white

sugar for dredging
mock cream for filling (see page 79)

1 Whisk egg whites until they are stiff enough to stand up in peaks.
2 Add a quarter of the sugar and whisk again until smooth and satiny looking.

3 Fold in rest of sugar with a metal spoon, quickly and lightly, lifting the mixture well up, but not beating.
4 With two wetted dessertspoons, shape the mixture into ovals on to a sheet of oiled, thick paper placed on a baking sheet.
5 Dredge the tops with castor sugar or sieved icing sugar.
6 Bake in a very cool oven (240°F.—Gas Mark ¼) for 2 hours, or until meringues are dry without browning.
7 After baking for 1½ hours turn the meringues carefully over with a broad, sharp knife, so that the under-side dries for the remaining half-hour.
8 When cold, store in air-tight tin. Serve with two ovals sandwiched together with mock cream or butter cream.

Note:
If preferred the meringue mixture can be piped using a bag with ½-inch nozzle, to make fancy shapes or to make spirals ending with a sharp point at the top.

Roll-out Biscuits
Basic Recipe

you will need:

6 oz. plain flour
2 oz. cornflour
good pinch salt
4 oz. butter or best margarine

3 oz. castor sugar
1 large egg yolk
½ teaspoon vanilla essence
little milk, if necessary

1 Sieve flour, cornflour and salt into basin.
2 Cream butter and sugar together until light and creamy.
3 Add beaten egg yolk to creamed mixture and mix well.
4 Work the dry mixture into the creamed mixture, adding vanilla essence at the same time.
5 When all dry mixture is worked in, knead with fingertips until a putty-like lump is formed, adding a little milk only if the mixture will not 'dough up'.
6 Roll the biscuit dough in greaseproof paper; place in fridge or very cold place until thoroughly chilled.
7 Roll out on sugared board to about ⅛-inch thickness.
8 Cut out with plain or fancy cutters; place on floured baking sheet.
9 Bake in moderate oven (355°F.—Gas Mark 4) until light brown – 12 to 15 minutes.

Variations:

Chocolate Biscuits: Use 2 oz. chocolate flavoured cornflour instead of plain flour.

Ginger Biscuits: Use ½ oz. powdered ginger and ½ oz. ground cinnamon and 1 oz. cornflour instead of 2 oz. cornflour.

Animal Biscuits: Cut out plain or chocolate mixture with animal cutters; mark features, buttons, collars, etc., with icing, using liner tube.

Decorated Biscuits: A little coloured or chocolate glacé icing (see page 79) can be spread on the biscuits after they have cooled, and a selection of chocolate dots, halved glacé cherries, hundreds and thousands, walnut halves and split blanched almonds can be fixed into the icing.
The biscuits can be brushed over with a little melted jam and sprinkled with chopped or flaked nuts.

Shortbread Biscuits

you will need:

6 oz. plain flour	5 oz. butter or best
1 oz. ground rice	margarine
4 oz. icing sugar	flour and castor sugar for
pinch salt	sprinkling

1 Sieve the dry ingredients together.
2 Rub in the fat until the mixture is crumbly.
3 Turn it out on to a board sprinkled with a mixture of flour and castor sugar.
4 With the fingers press the mixture until it blends and becomes putty-like. *Add no moisture;* warmth of fingers is sufficient to soften the fat.
5 Wrap in greaseproof paper and leave in fridge to get thoroughly cold and firm.
6 Roll out on a board sprinkled with castor sugar to just less than ¼-inch thickness.
7 Cut out with jimpy edged pastry cutter or fancy cutters; squeeze the scraps together after cutting, roll out again and cut out.
8 Place on tin covered with greaseproof paper; prick each biscuit with a fork.
9 Bake in moderate oven (355°F.—Gas Mark 4), until golden brown – 15 to 20 minutes.
10 Sprinkle with castor sugar; store in tin when cold.

Petticoat Tails: Roll out shortbread mixture into a round about the size of a pudding plate. Neaten edges, then pinch with finger and thumb. Cut out centre with large, plain pastry cutter; lay it on baking sheet. Divide the ring left into 8 triangles; lay on baking sheet; bake 40 to 50 minutes; sprinkle with sugar. Serve with circle in middle and Petticoat Tails arranged around.

Daddies' Cookies

you will need:

2 oz. butter or margarine	2 oz. quick rolled oats
2 oz. soft brown sugar	2½ oz. flour
1 tablespoon water	½ teaspoon bicarbonate
1 tablespoon syrup	soda

1 Melt the fat with the sugar; add water and syrup.
2 Mix the dry ingredients and stir into the syrup mixture.
3 Roll into balls about the size of a walnut.
4 Bake in moderate oven (355°F.—Gas Mark 4) 12 to 15 minutes. Space the cookies well apart on baking sheet, as they spread in baking.
Variations:
Add 1 oz. chocolate dots to the mixture with dry ingredients.
Add 1 oz. cleaned currants with the dry ingredients.
Brush tops with milk and sprinkle with desiccated coconut as soon as cookies are baked.
Put half a walnut on top of each, or sprinkle with chopped walnuts or almonds as soon as they are taken from oven, pressing them on lightly.

Drop Cookies – Basic Mixture

you will need:

8 oz. plain flour	3 oz. castor sugar
½ teaspoon baking powder	1 beaten egg
pinch salt	2–3 tablespoons milk
3 oz. butter, margarine or	¼ teaspoon vanilla essence
cooking fat	

1 Sieve flour, baking powder and salt together.
2 Cream fat and sugar, add beaten egg, beat until light and frothy.
3 Add dry mixture to creamed mixture alternately with the milk, until a stiff, rocky mixture is formed.

4 Do not allow it to get too soft; when dropped on baking sheet it should hold its shape in a pile.
5 Add essence last and mix well.
6 Drop teaspoons of mixture on greased baking sheet, spacing well apart.
7 Bake in fairly hot oven (400°F.—Gas Mark 6) 12–15 minutes; allow to set a little on tray before removing.

Fruit and Nut Cookies: Add 3 oz. mixed dried fruit and 1 oz. chopped nuts to the mixture.

Chocolate Chip Cookies: Omit 1 tablespoon flour and use the same amount of sweetened chocolate powder instead. Decorate tops with chocolate drops or dots, fixed on with a little glacé icing.

Spiced Cookies: Add 1 teaspoon mixed cake spice to the mixture.

Almond Drops: Use 6 oz. flour and 2 oz. ground almonds, and substitute almond essence for vanilla. Put $\frac{1}{4}$ shelled almond on top of each.

Icings & Fillings

Glacé Icing

8 oz. icing sugar $\frac{1}{8}$ pint tepid water

Sieve sugar, add water gradually until mixture coats back of spoon; do not beat.

Coloured Icing

Add a few drops vegetable colouring during the mixing, a drop at a time, using less water if necessary.

Orange or Lemon Glacé Icing

Substitute strained orange or lemon juice for the water; if necessary add a few drops yellow or orange colouring.

Coffee Glacé Icing

8 oz. icing sugar $1\frac{1}{2}$ tablespoons water
$\frac{1}{2}$ tablespoon coffee essence

Make as for white Glacé Icing.

Chocolate Glacé Icing

2 oz. plain chocolate   8 oz. icing sugar
slightly less than $\frac{1}{2}$ teaspoon vanilla
$\frac{1}{4}$ pint water $\frac{1}{4}$ oz. butter

Dissolve chocolate in water without boiling; cool, add sieved icing sugar and vanilla; stir until sugar dissolves. Add butter and a little more water if necessary.

American Icing

1 lb. loaf sugar   2 egg whites
$\frac{1}{4}$ pint water

1 Dissolve sugar in water; boil until syrupy.
2 Whisk egg whites stiffly; whisk syrup slowly on to whites.
3 Continue whisking until mixture begins to thicken and leaves a trail; pour over cake at once.
Colouring may be used; add during whisking.

Fillings
Mock Cream (1)

you will need:

$\frac{1}{2}$ oz. cornflour   2 oz. sieved icing sugar
$\frac{1}{4}$ pint milk   flavouring
2 oz. butter or best margarine

1 Blend cornflour with a little milk, boil rest, add blended cornflour, and stir until boiling. Leave to cool.
2 Cream fat and sugar together.
3 Whisk almost cold sauce into creamed mixture a teaspoon at a time. Add flavouring during whisking.

Mock Cream (2)

you will need:

1 can evaporated milk   2 tablespoons warm water
1 tablespoon icing sugar   flavouring essence
$\frac{1}{2}$ oz. powder gelatine

1 Put the can of milk in pan with cold water to cover.
2 Bring to the boil; boil 10 minutes; leave overnight.
3 Turn milk into basin; whisk until stiff.
4 Add sugar and few drops flavouring, blending well.
5 Dissolve gelatine in water; stir into the cream.
6 Cool in fridge; use for cake filling, and for spreading on tops.

Confectioner's Custard

you will need:

½ pint milk
2 oz. cornflour
2 oz. butter or best
  margarine
1 large egg yolk, or
  2 small

1½ oz. castor sugar
½ teaspoon vanilla essence
1 tablespoon cream from
  top of milk, or
  evaporated milk

1 Make a thick sauce with milk, flour and fat (see page 50).
2 Add yolk of egg, sugar and vanilla.
3 Return to heat and cook gently until thickened; do not boil.
4 Cool; add cream.
5 When quite cold, use as a filling between sandwich cakes and biscuits.
Custard Powder may be used instead of cornflour, or the custard may be coloured with a few drops yellow colouring. 1–2 oz. chopped glacé fruits and nuts may be added for sandwich or layer cake filling.

Ring Doughnuts

you will need:

12 oz. self-raising flour
¼ teaspoon salt
2 tablespoons castor sugar
2 oz. butter or best
  margarine
2 eggs (standard size)
about 4 tablespoons milk

¼ teaspoon vanilla essence
deep fat or oil for frying
castor sugar for sprinkling

1 Sieve flour, salt and sugar into bowl.
2 Melt butter or margarine and stir it in.
3 Add the beaten eggs and mix thoroughly, then add milk to make a stiff dough. Work in vanilla essence.
4 Turn the mixture on to a floured board and work until quite smooth.
5 Roll out to ½-inch thickness.
6 Cut into rounds with a 2½-inch plain cutter. Cut out centres of these with a 1½-inch cutter.
7 Re-roll these centres with trimmings of dough and cut out until all dough is used.
8 Have ready pan of deep hot fat; drop the rings in carefully. Do not allow them to touch; leave room for swelling. Not more than 3 or 4 should be fried at once.
9 Rings will rise to top of fat; cook until beginning to turn golden. Turn over and finish cooking, until well risen and golden brown – about 4 minutes.
10 Take up with perforated spoon on to absorbent paper. Sprinkle with sugar. Leave until quite cold; eat at once or store in tin.
This quantity makes 20 to 24 doughnuts.

Jam Doughnuts: Break off small pieces of the dough; form into balls about the size of golf balls. Flatten with the fingers, make a slight indentation in middle. Put half a teaspoon of strawberry or raspberry jam in the hollow, pull the outer edge of round up over the jam, pinching it well. Roll on lightly floured board to make a good shape, then put doughnuts into the hot fat. Cook until brown all over, turning often. The round doughnuts will take a little longer to cook than the ring doughnuts; lower heat under the pan as soon as they begin to brown so they can cook through without over-browning. Take up with draining spoon on to absorbent paper; sprinkle with castor sugar and eat hot or cold.

Preserves, Pickles and Chutneys

I think we all agree that the prices of jams, marmalades, pickles, chutneys and bottled sauces are so high these days as to make them luxuries. Especially if you have to feed a family on a small budget. A pound pot of jam seems to go no way at all, and pickles and chutneys are out of the question as regular items on the dinner or supper table. Yet they do help to make meals interesting; the dullest piece of left-over meat is given a lift with a spicy pickle or chutney to accompany it.

So why not try to make your own? Many of the ingredients for preserves and pickles are quite inexpensive if you buy the fruits and vegetables when they are in season, and keep an eye open for bargains – bruised apples going cheaply, or windfalls; rhubarb at the end of the season while not very good for pies or for stewing, makes excellent chutney. Watch out for the small pickling onions or shallots when they come along; they are not in the shops for long, but you'll get 2 lb. of pickled onions for less than half-a-crown. And what about marrows, so cheap at the height of the season – and cauliflower or broccoli? With a few of those onions added you can make an excellent piccalilli better than you buy in the shops, at about a quarter of the price.

Tips About Pickling

1 Only the best malt or spirit vinegar should be used (not the acetic acid type), fresh spices, coarse salt (not the 'refined' table salt).
2 The term 'Mixed Pickling Spice' is rather vague; usually it consists of cloves, whole allspice, mustard seed, peppercorns, chillis, blade mace, root ginger; really it is better to buy these separately, and mix them to make your pickles or chutneys as hot or aromatic as you like.
3 All vinegar must be boiled with the spices long enough to get the flavour of the spices; the spices themselves should not be put in the jars, though a few red chillis in a jar of clear pickles look pretty through the glass.
4 Don't attempt to make pickles of any kind without first boiling the vinegar, even if you prefer it unspiced; unboiled vinegar will soon turn bad.
5 Stainless steel or enamel pans should be used for boiling vinegar; never copper, brass or iron.
6 Vegetables should be brined overnight before pickling; salt extracts excess water, is absorbed by the vegetables and acts as a preservative as well as seasoning.
7 If a crisp pickle is preferred in the case of onions, clear mixed vegetables, cucumber, use the spiced vinegar cold; if a soft pickle is wanted, use vinegar hot.

Spiced Vinegar

you will need:

1 quart best malt vinegar	$\frac{1}{2}$ oz. bruised root ginger
1 oz. peppercorns	$\frac{1}{4}$ oz. mustard seed
$\frac{1}{2}$ oz. whole allspice	6 bay leaves
$\frac{1}{2}$ oz. blade mace	$\frac{1}{4}$ oz. coriander seeds
$\frac{1}{4}$ oz. cloves	4–6 chillis
2-inch strip stick cinnamon	

1 Put vinegar and spices on to boil; boil 3–4 minutes.
2 Allow vinegar to go cold with spices in it; if the vinegar is not to be used at once, pour it off into a jug, with the spices in it.
3 Strain when required for pickling; use vinegar hot when soft, raw vegetable pickle is required; cold if crisp pickle is preferred.
4 A few of the seeds and one or two chillis may be put on top of pickles in jars, but don't mix them in with the pickles.
Note:
When a white pickle is required such as small white onions (known as 'Silverskin' or cocktail onions) or cauliflower, white malt vinegar should be used, and cloves, allspice and black peppercorns should be omitted as they are apt to stain the vegetables.
Never boil vinegar too long: it evaporates.

Pickled Cabbage

you will need:

2 lb. red cabbage	$\frac{3}{4}$—1 pint cold spiced vinegar
3–4 tablespoons coarse salt	

1 Remove outer leaves from cabbage, wash and quarter.
2 Remove hard centre stalk; shred cabbage finely across the leaves.
3 Spread cut cabbage on a shallow dish, sprinkling salt among it.
4 Put a final good layer of salt over top of cabbage. Leave overnight.
5 Drain off liquid from cabbage; shake it well in a colander.
6 Pack, not too tightly, into glass jars; cover with the vinegar.
7 Allow time for vinegar to seep through the cabbage, then top it up with more vinegar which should reach at least $\frac{1}{2}$ inch above cabbage.
8 Tie down; keep at least 14 days before using.
Note:
Ordinary jam jars are quite suitable to use for pickles, and plain white, or waxed paper, fastened down with string or rubber bands can be used. It is most important to avoid any kind of metal coming in contact with the vinegar, so screw-bands are not recommended.
It is difficult to give the exact amount of vinegar that will be required to well cover the cabbage and allow the extra $\frac{1}{2}$ inch at the top, so allow more if necessary; the cabbage absorbs vinegar the longer it is kept.

Pickled Onions or Shallots

you will need:

2 lb. pickling onions or shallots	1 quart spiced vinegar
2–3 tablespoons coarse salt	

1 Peel the onions (which should be as even sized as possible).
2 Spread on shallow dish, sprinkling salt among them.
3 Sprinkle a good layer of salt on top; leave overnight.
4 Put the onions through a colander to drain off liquid.
5 Pack them, not too tightly, into jars; arrange the onions with handle of wooden spoon so there are no large spaces.
6 Cover with spiced vinegar – cold for a crisp pickle, hot for a fairly soft pickle.
7 Tie down. If hot vinegar is used let it cool before tying down. A few of the spices may be sprinkled on top.
8 Keep 3 to 4 weeks before using.

Clear Mixed Pickles

you will need:

1 lb. shallots or small pickling onions
1 lb. cauliflower
1 medium sized cucumber or 2 ridge cucumbers

2–3 tablespoons coarse salt
3 pints spiced vinegar

1 Peel shallots or onions; break cauliflower into fairly small sprigs, rejecting the hard bottom stalk, though centre stalk can be used.
2 Wipe cucumber, cut off stalk end, cut cucumber into cubes, roughly the size of the onions.
3 Mix the vegetables, spread on a dish, sprinkling with coarse salt; put a good sprinkling of salt on top.
4 Leave overnight, then drain liquid away.
5 Pack in layers in jars, using wooden spoon handle to arrange them.
6 Cover with cold spiced vinegar. Put a few spices and a chilli or two on top.
7 Cover jars; keep several weeks before using.

Note:
An attractive white pickle can be made by using white malt vinegar, omitting cloves and black peppercorns; the cucumber should be peeled in this case.

Vegetable Marrow, peeled and seeded, can be included; increase quantity of salt and vinegar if necessary.

Marrow and Apple Chutney (1)

you will need:

3 lb. marrow, after peeling and seeding
1½ lb. onions
2 tablespoons coarse salt

2 lb. apples, after peeling, coring and removing bruised parts
1½ lb. brown sugar
3 pints spiced vinegar

1 Cut the marrow into slices after peeling and seeding; peel and chop onions.
2 Put marrow and onions on shallow dish, sprinkling with coarse salt; leave 24 hours, then drain.
3 Peel, core and slice apples, put in pan with marrow and onions, and sugar.
4 Cook in half the vinegar until tender and apples form a 'mush', stirring from time to time.
5 Add remaining vinegar and simmer until reduced and thickened.

6 Pot up while still hot and cover at once. Ready to eat immediately.

Note:
As this is a thick pickle it is not wise to put any of the pickling spices in the jars; it would be hard to avoid them when eating the chutney. Windfall apples can well be used for chutney making, so long as they are of the cooking variety.

Fruity Chutney

you will need:

1 lb. seedless raisins
8 oz. cooking dates, chopped small
8 oz. currants
3 large onions, chopped

1 oz. chillis, crushed
2 oz. bruised root ginger
4 lb. apples, after preparation
2 lb. Demerara sugar
3 pints vinegar

1 Put all the fruit in pan with the vinegar; add chillis and ginger wrapped in muslin.
2 Simmer until the apples are mushy, stirring often.
3 Remove the chillis and ginger.
4 Add the sugar; boil about 10 minutes longer, until chutney thickens. Stir often to prevent sticking.

Note:
These quantities give 8 to 10 lb. mild chutney; if a hotter chutney is liked, use spiced vinegar.

Dried Apricot Chutney

you will need:

8 oz. dried apricots, cut small and soaked all night in 1 pint vinegar
1 lb. tart apples, after peeling coring and removing bruises
1 lb. seedless raisins

1 lb. chopped onions
½ teaspoon cayenne pepper
½ teaspoon ground ginger
½ teaspoon salt
2 teaspoons mustard
1½ lb. soft brown sugar

1 Put apricots and vinegar in which they were soaked in pan.
2 Bring to the boil, then add remaining ingredients except sugar.

3 When chutney has cooked for 15 minutes, add the sugar and continue cooking until apricots, onions and raisins are tender, and apples mushy, stirring often.

4 Pour into hot jars; tie down at once. Ready for eating as soon as cold.

Rhubarb Chutney: Substitute same weight of young, juicy rhubarb after removing skin and root ends; cut into 1-inch pieces. Add 1 oz. bruised root ginger, and yellow skin of 1 lemon (tied in muslin and removed after cooking), and the juice of the lemon.

Green Tomato Chutney

you will need:

4 lb. green tomatoes	8 oz. seedless raisins
1 lb. cooking apples, after preparation	½ oz. root ginger
	12 chillis
1½ lb. shallots or pickling onions	1 lb. soft brown sugar
	1 pint vinegar

1 Slice tomatoes, cut up apples and shallots or onions, chop raisins.

2 Bruise the ginger and the chillis, tie in muslin.

3 Place all ingredients in pan; simmer gently until vegetables are cooked and the chutney thickens.

4 Remove the bag of ginger and chillis; bottle chutney in hot jars. Cover at once.

Apple Chutney

you will need:

4 lb. tart cooking apples, after preparation	1 lb. onions, chopped
8 oz. seedless raisins	1 lb. soft brown sugar
8 oz. currants	1 oz. mustard seed
8 oz. cooking dates, chopped	1 oz. salt
	3–4 pints vinegar (to well-cover ingredients)

1 Put all ingredients in pan together, stir well and bring to the boil.

2 Simmer 45 minutes to 1 hour, until reduced to thick mush, stirring from time to time.

3 Pour into hot jars; tie down at once.

Note: Windfall apples may be used for chutney provided all bruised parts are cut away; chutneys, being cooked pickles, can be used immediately, though they mature with keeping.

Marrow and Apple Chutney (2)

you will need:

4 lb. marrow after peeling and seeding	2 lb. cooking apples, after preparation
1½ lb. onions, chopped	1½ lb. soft brown sugar
coarse salt	2 pints spiced vinegar

1 Cut marrow into slices, after peeling and removing seeds.

2 Spread marrow and onions on shallow dish, sprinkle with salt and leave overnight.

3 Peel and core apples, removing all bruises, and cut into thin slices.

4 Drain liquid from marrow and onions; put all ingredients in pan and simmer until thickened, stirring often.

5 Pour into heated jars; tie down at once.

Date and Apple Chutney

you will need:

2 lb. cooking dates, stoned	1 level teaspoon salt
2 medium sized onions	1 level teaspoon dry mustard
2 lb. cooking apples, after peeling and coring	1 level teaspoon ground ginger
8 oz. brown sugar	1 pint spiced vinegar

1 Chop dates coarsely; peel and chop onions; slice apples.

2 Place in large saucepan; add sugar, salt, mustard and ginger; mix well together.

3 Add the vinegar, stir well, simmer gently for 1 hour or until thickened.

4 Pour into hot jars; cover at once with white waxed paper or polythene.

Note:
Rhubarb may be substituted for apples. If a milder chutney is preferred, use plain vinegar. These quantities yield 6 to 7 lb. chutney.

Dried Apricot Jam

you will need:

1 lb. dried apricots	1 oz. blanched and
3 pints water	shredded almonds
3 lb. sugar	juice of 1 lemon

1 Wash apricots, cut them into quarters.
2 Put in saucepan with the water; soak overnight.
3 Cook for 20 minutes, or until apricots are tender.
4 Add sugar, stir without boiling until sugar dissolves, bring to the boil.
5 Add shredded almonds and lemon juice; boil quickly until jam sets when tested on cold plate.
6 Pour into heated jars; tie down when cold.

Note:
This is a very useful jam, as it can be made any time of the year; these quantities give 6 lb. jam.

Gooseberry and Strawberry Jam

you will need:

1 lb. green gooseberries	2 lb. strawberries
water to just cover	3 lb. sugar
gooseberries	

1 Top and tail gooseberries; wash them, cut in halves, and put in pan with water to just cover.
2 Simmer until tender, stirring well, and pressing berries to sides of pan.
3 Add the stalked and wiped strawberries (avoid washing), and stir and simmer a further 5–8 minutes. Large berries should be halved.
4 Add the sugar, stir over low heat, without boiling, until sugar is dissolved, then boil rapidly until a good set is reached – about 10 minutes.
5 Pour into hot jars; tie down at once or leave until quite cold.

Note:
Young Rhubarb may be used instead of gooseberries; it should be skinned and root ends removed, and cut up small.

Raspberries can be substituted for strawberries.

Gooseberry Jam

you will need:

3 lb. green gooseberries	3 lb. sugar
¾ pint water	

1 Top and tail gooseberries, wash them and place in pan with water.
2 Simmer for 20 minutes, or until berries are tender without being actually broken down.
3 Add warmed sugar, stir over low heat until sugar dissolves.
4 Boil rapidly until jam turns faintly pink and a little tested on cold plate sets when cold.
5 Pour into heated jars and tie down immediately.

Rhubarb and Pineapple Jam

you will need:

4 lb. rhubarb	12 oz. can pineapple
3 lb. sugar	pieces
2 lemons, grated rind and	
juice	

1 Wash rhubarb, keep skin on but remove root ends, cut up small.
2 Place in saucepan, with just sufficient water to prevent sticking.
3 When rhubarb is soft, add sugar, grated lemon rind and juice, and pineapple pieces.
4 Boil fast for about 20 minutes, stirring often, until setting point is reached. (Test on cold plate.)
5 Pour into heated jars and tie down.

Note:
Weights of tins of pineapple vary between 10, 12 or 16 oz.; a 10 oz. can would be sufficient, but a little would have to be removed from a 16 oz. can.
If pineapple pieces are not available, rings or chunks can be chopped and used instead.

Lemon Curd

you will need:

4 oz. butter	grated rind and juice of
8 oz. granulated sugar	2 lemons
3 eggs	

1 Melt butter in top part of double boiler, placed over low heat.

2 Add sugar slowly and stir until well blended.
3 Beat eggs and pour them gradually into melted butter and sugar.
4 Stir until mixture is light and creamy; do not allow it to get very hot.
5 Add grated lemon peel and strained juice slowly, stirring all the time.
6 Place the pan over lower part of double saucepan filled with boiling water.
7 Turn heat to low, to keep the water just boiling. Stir until curd forms a film over back of spoon.
8 Pour into heated jar; cover securely with waxed or grease-proof paper immediately.

Note:
These quantities are sufficient to fill a 1-lb. jar; Lemon Curd will keep approximately 6 weeks; it is better to make a small quantity at a time.

Gooseberry, Apple and Rhubarb Jam

you will need:

1½ lb. green gooseberries	2 pints water
1½ lb. rhubarb	5 lb. sugar
1 lb. cooking apples, after peeling and coring	

1 Top and tail gooseberries, wipe and chop rhubarb into small pieces; peel, core and chop apples.
2 Put fruit in pan with water, bring to the boil and simmer until tender – 20 to 30 minutes.
3 Add sugar, stir until sugar is dissolved, then boil quickly for about 15 minutes. Test on cold plate for setting point.
4 Pour off into heated jars; tie down at once, or when quite cold.

Marrow Ginger

you will need:

2 lb. peeled marrow	1 lemon
1 pint water	1 oz. preserved ginger
2 lb. sugar	in syrup
2 oz. bruised root ginger	

1 Cut the marrow into small cubes.

2 Boil sugar and water together until syrupy.
3 Add ginger to the syrup with the grated rind and juice of lemon.
4 Put in the marrow and boil until marrow looks clear and is tender. Remove the root ginger.
5 Drain off the syrup, add the chopped preserved ginger and syrup from it.
6 Boil up again, then add the marrow, and boil rapidly until syrup jells when tested on cold plate.
7 Divide the marrow equally between heated jars and fill up with the syrup. Tie down at once.

Note:
This is more than a jam, and can be served as a dessert with cream, or without.
The preserved ginger can be omitted, but is a great improvement.

Year-Round Marmalade

you will need:

1 lb. grapefruit	4 pints water
3 lemons	4 lb. sugar
1 lb. sweet oranges	

1 Wash fruit well and peel it; cut peel into shreds, removing some pith if very thick.
2 Slice fruit coarsely, removing pips and pith; remove as much skin as possible between sections of grapefruit.
3 Tie pips, skin and pith in muslin bag. Put rinds, fruit pulp and any juice squeezed out into large bowl; add pips, etc. Pour in water, leave 24 hours.
4 Put all into preserving pan; simmer gently until peel is tender – 1 to 1½ hours, and liquid has reduced to about half.
5 Remove bag of pips, pressing to expel all liquid.
6 Add heated sugar, stir over low heat until sugar dissolves, then boil quickly until setting point is reached – about 20 minutes.
7 Allow marmalade to stand in pan when done for a few minutes, stirring once or twice, then pour into heated jars.
8 Put a wax disc on top of marmalade and tie down at once, or leave until quite cold.

Note:
This is a sweet, coarse marmalade; when Seville oranges are in season, they can be substituted for sweet oranges, if preferred.

Gooseberry Mint Jelly

you will need:

2 lb. green gooseberries
sugar

½ pint measure chopped
mint
½ pint vinegar

1 Top and tail gooseberries, halve them and cook them in just sufficient water to prevent sticking, until reduced to a pulp.
2 Press the gooseberry pulp well against sides of pan, then strain it through a flannel or muslin bag.
3 Allow juice to drip overnight, then measure it and allow 1 lb. sugar to each pint.
4 Put juice and sugar in pan with the vinegar and the mint, stir until sugar melts.
5 Boil steadily until a good set is reached when a little is tested on a cold plate.
6 When done let it stand in the pan for a minute or two, then stir well to disperse the mint evenly.
7 Pour into small pots; tie down at once, or leave to go quite cold.

Note:

This is an excellent substitute for Mint Sauce during the winter, especially with cold lamb or mutton.
Apple or **Rhubarb** juice may be used instead of gooseberries; add the juice of a lemon if rhubarb juice is used, to help the setting.

Damson Cheese

you will need:

Damsons

1 lb. sugar to 1 lb. pulp

1 Stalk and wash as many damsons as you have. Put them in a stone jar or casserole, cover and place in a slow oven until juice runs, and stones are easily removed.
2 Stir well; rub fruit through a sieve. Remove kernels from stones and add them to the pulp.
3 Measure pulp and heat required amount of sugar. Mix sugar with pulp and put in a pan.
4 Boil until it jells when tested, then pour into small jars.
5 Put paper dipped in brandy (if possible) on top of each and tie down at once. Keep for six months before using it.

The cheese will shrink a little from sides of jars and have a crust of sugar. Instead of putting brandied paper on top, a bay leaf can be put on top of the cheese before tying down.

INDEX